PRACTICAL
SCROLLSAW
PATTERNS

PRACTICAL
SCROLLSAW
PATTERNS

John Everett

Guild of Master Craftsman Publications Ltd

First published 2000 by
Guild of Master Craftsman Publications Ltd
166 High Street, Lewes
East Sussex, BN7 1XU

ISBN 1 86108 162 6

Cover design by Graham Willmott, GMC Design Studio
Book design by Fineline Studios
Typeface: Officina Sans

Colour Separation by Viscan Graphics Pte Ltd (Singapore)
Printed in China by Sun Fung Offset Binding Co., Ltd.

Measurements

Throughout this book instances may be found where a metric measurement has fractionally varying imperial equivalents, usually within $\frac{1}{16}$in either way. This is because in each particular case the closest imperial equivalent has been given.

A mixture of metric and imperial measurements should NEVER be used – always use either one of the other.

See also metric conversion table on page 113.

Contents

PROJECTS

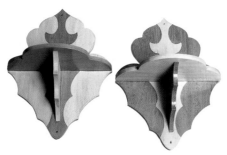

Introduction

People already familiar with the scrollsaw will not need telling just what a versatile piece of equipment it is. It can cope with a wide range of cutting jobs, from the basic cutting out of outlines in blocks of timber prior to final carving, to incredibly intricate patterns in a vast range of materials, such as sheet gold and silver for jewellery, providing you follow the proper procedures when working with materials other than wood.

There is a huge range of blades available for the scrollsaw, and they are available virtually anywhere in the world. By selecting the appropriate type of blade, the scrollsaw can make woodworking joints, such as mortice and tenon and peg joints, easily and accurately; it can also cut difficult materials, such as plywood, cleanly, if a reverse-tooth blade, with its lower teeth set backwards, is used; this will prevent the splintering effect encountered with standard blades, as the saw cuts on the up stroke for the bottom part of its cutting range.

Spiral blades, which cut in all directions, are useful too, as they permit even a small scrollsaw to cut relatively large sheets of material: the workpiece can simply be moved in any direction to follow the cutting pattern lines, without rotating the workpiece.

I have assumed that the scrollsaw most people will have to hand will be the standard 16in (406mm) throat type or smaller, so you will not need a huge industrial machine to cope with all the patterns designed especially for this book. In fact the patterns have been carefully selected so that only the very minimum number of tools is needed, and little equipment.

Most of the patterns can be easily adapted to suit your own preferences, both in terms of size and the type of material used to construct them. For example, you may well have a piece of prized timber you are waiting to use, or you may wish to make up a design to fit in a particular space in your home. Whatever your individual needs, these patterns can be adapted to fit.

When you are ready to begin a project, read through the text and familiarize yourself with what will be needed to complete it. Not only will this save you time later on, but it will help you to avoid making inconvenient errors. Once you are happy that you have a clear image in your mind of what you need to do, you should have no difficulty in successfully completing your chosen project.

John Everett

Materials

Various materials can be used on the scrollsaw. Wood and wood-based man-made sheet material are of course the most obvious and these are used most frequently for scrollsaw projects. They include hard- and softwoods, ply in all its variations and MDF (medium density fibreboard), which is now readily available in a wide variety of thicknesses and grades.

Hardwood

Some hardwoods, such as oak, may have been fully cured some years prior to being used, so will have become extremely hard indeed. In this case, it would be better to use a metal-cutting blade rather than a standard variety.

Softwood

Some pines and hemlocks are so soft that they leave a fibrous finish once sawn. So bear in mind that with these types of timber, careful sanding, particularly on the cut edges, may be required to get a smooth finish.

MDF

This is a very versatile product. As with chipboard and other particle boards, fixing screws can be a problem, but this can often be overcome by using two different fixing methods, e.g. glue and screws, or glue and pins, or indeed, by arranging things so that the fixings pass through the MDF and are secured into parts made from regular timber.

One of the advantages of MDF is the clean edge left on the material after cutting which

Jigsaw puzzle piece and initial letter 'J' cut from slate, to demonstrate what can be achieved on the scrollsaw from a piece of broken slate

means that, generally, MDF doesn't require any sanding, other than cleaning off saw tearout. This is a tremendous advantage when cutting intricate and detailed work, which would be almost impossible to sand. In addition, the face sides of MDF boards provide an adequate surface which does not need sanding and, as with other sheet material of this sort, it has no grain and so will cut easily and at the same speed in any direction.

Remember, however, that MDF can be toxic and it is essential to take safety precautions (see 'The dangers of sawdust' on page 4).

To show how versatile the scrollsaw can be, a couple of the patterns in this book have been made using alternative materials: the key rack (see pattern on page 29) was made from a scrap sheet of 3mm (⅛in) thick mild steel, and the top plates of the candle holders (see pattern on page 65) were made from pieces of salvaged roofing slate.

A selection of natural and man-made woods. From the bottom up: oak, mahogany, pine board, MDF and plywood

Safety

Common sense

The most important thing to remember is to use your common sense. The blades used in the scrollsaw or fretsaw are thin with tiny teeth, and these teeth are capable of cutting through thick, hard materials. It therefore follows that, small though the teeth are, they are also capable of cutting through a finger or thumb. It is essential to keep an eye on where your fingers are in relation to the saw blade you are using.

Blade breakage

Most scrollsaw accidents occur when a scrollsaw-user applies too much pressure to the workpiece, in an endeavour to cut faster, and the blade breaks. Blades for the scrollsaw are not expensive so, if you find you need pressure to make the blade cut through your workpiece, change the blade. A replacement blade is considerably cheaper than a week or two off work with a damaged finger.

Protect your eyes

It is important to wear safety goggles at all times when cutting unfamiliar materials, and whenever working stone, slate or metals. It may be a nuisance wearing them, but remember the slight inconvenience is nothing compared to the prospect of living with permanently damaged eyes. There are so many makes and type of goggles/safety glasses available cheaply, that it is well worth trying a few, to see which suits you best.

The dangers of sawdust

The scrollsaw produces very fine sawdust that can remain suspended in the air for quite some time. This can be a particular problem to those who suffer from asthma and other respiratory tract problems. In addition, some materials, including a few hardwoods and some man-made sheet materials such as MDF, produce dust which is toxic (although there is now a formaldehyde-free range of MDF).

The importance of dust masks

Many scrollsaws have a dust extraction facility underneath the saw table; this is helpful but unfortunately not the complete answer, as there will always be dust produced above the saw table. To counteract this, most saws also have an air blower to keep the line on your cutting pattern free of sawdust, but this blows the ultra-fine dust into the air around you. Because of this, a dust mask must always be worn when cutting with the scrollsaw. There are many dust masks available in DIY stores and garages, so spend a little time finding one that you find comfortable to wear. Preventing damage is, after all, better than cure.

Cleaning up

Never use a dustpan and brush to clean up after cutting with your scrollsaw – it will simply spread the dust. Always vacuum up as much dust as possible. A build-up of fine dust can clog the working parts of your scrollsaw and, by applying good housekeeping rules, you can prevent such problems from occurring too often. See also 'Safety note' on page 7.

Scrollsaw basics

Scaling a pattern up or down

You can do this on a photocopier, or you can scale up the template using a grid. When the grid pattern is based on, say, a one centimetre grid, to create a 200% enlargement (double the original size) you would need to copy the template shape onto a two centimetre grid.

If you number the rows of grids on both the original and the copy, it will be easier to find your place quickly.

Put a dot at each point where the cutting line crosses from one square to another. All you then have to do is join the dots, ensuring any curves follow the line of the original.

Sketch in the design first with a light pencil, to ensure you get the drawing exactly right before you are committed to an ink line.

Take your time to make a satisfactory cutting pattern, as the quality of the finished item will depend on the accuracy of this template.

Attaching a cutting pattern

Attach the cutting pattern using an adhesive, such as spray mount or other low tack adhesive. This will allow the remains of the cutting pattern to be easily removed from the blank once cutting has been completed.

With a little practice you will get the hang of using spray adhesive and find it fairly easy to apply. Just remember that if you use too much adhesive when sticking the pattern to much adhesive when sticking the pattern to the blank, removing the pattern will prove messy, while too little adhesive will mean that the pattern won't stick properly.

Making a blank

A blank is a plainly cut piece of wood or other material. It is usually cut a little larger than the size of the cutting pattern, so that there is some spare material which can be gripped, to control the direction of the cut.

To make the blank, select the material you intend to use and place the cutting pattern on it so that it does not waste too much material. Draw around the outside of the cutting pattern – not too closely – so that the marked area is a little larger than the template. Cut the blank free from its sheet with a saw. A jigsaw is useful for this if you have one, but any other suitable saw will do just as well. Finally, sand off the edges of the material so that there is no saw tearout.

Setting up the scrollsaw

Before you start, make sure your scrollsaw is set up properly. Check that it is firmly bolted to the bench and that the cables and plug are not damaged in any way, such as nicks in the insulation.

Some scrollsaws have an optional stand. This is a useful facility as it prevents your workbench space being taken up with tools and equipment. Some stands also have a built-in swivel chair for the operator. Whatever arrangement you have, make sure you are comfortable and relaxed.

The hold-down device helps to keep the workpiece flat on the table, preventing 'chattering' when you turn corners with the saw. Make sure you set the hold-down device correctly before starting to saw.

The tension of the blade must be adjusted before you begin sawing. If the blade is too tight, there is a risk of breakage, too loose and the sawing line could become inaccurate. See the manufacturer's manual for details of how to adjust the tension on your saw.

Basic cutting

Cutting with the scrollsaw is simple and you'll find you will improve with practice. Keep your eye on the point where the saw blade meets the cutting line and just follow the line. After a while you will be able to cut perfect straight lines and gentle curves, as well as tight turns.

Stack sawing

Two or more identical pieces can be cut by a process known as stack sawing. Two or more blanks are simply fixed together (usually with double-sided adhesive tape) and sawn around at the same time. This makes the job easier to complete, and ensures that all the pieces are identical.

Just cut out the required number of blanks and stick them together with little pieces of double-sided adhesive tape on the waste side of the cutting line. Attach the cutting pattern to the top of the blank, and cut around the cutting pattern. You may find that the blade cuts slightly slower because of the thickness of the material, but try not to force the material into the blade.

Internal cutouts

An internal cutout is a part of a pattern that needs to be cut away, but does not meet any of the edges. The cutout often forms part of the ornamentation of the piece.

To make an internal cutout, you will need to drill a hole for the saw blade to pass through. If small, delicate cutouts are required, then you will need to use a drill bit only slightly larger than the width of your blade. If the cutout is not delicate, use a large drill bit, to make threading the saw blades easier. Put a scrap of wood behind the hole position when you drill so you leave a clean edge at the back of the hole. This is particularly important if you are using plywood, as the splintering that can occur could spoil the final piece. Try to drill the starter holes near a sharp point or angle on the design. This will make it easier to ensure that the beginning and end of the cut meet up easily. If you were to begin your cutting line along a straight or gently curving section of the pattern, the start and finish of the cut might not meet exactly, making intricate filing or sanding necessary to make the cutting line meet precisely.

Secure the blade in the saw's bottom blade holder first. Thread the blade through your starter hole, secure the blade in the top blade holder and tension it properly. Check the manufacturer's handbook for the particular tensioning arrangement for your saw.

It is usually better to complete the internal cutouts first. This will ensure that there is enough waste material to grip when guiding the blank along the cutting line.

Finishing

There are many possible wood finishes but, for the projects in this book, we need only concern ourselves with paint finishes, enamels, wood stains and varnishes.

Paint undercoat

Whatever type of paint you are using, most woods, natural or artificial, will require some form of undercoat in order to get the best finish. The use of a primer is not only an advantage, but in the case of some artificial materials such as MDF, virtually essential to obtain even paint coverage. A white primer not only seals the wood prior to painting, so that the wood does not absorb too much paint, it also provides a degree of light reflection through the top coat of paint, giving the colour coat a brighter appearance.

Another advantage of using primer, particularly with softwoods and MDF, is that it renders immobile, and therefore removable with sandpaper, those annoying little bits that need to be sanded off but cannot be removed by sandpaper while the wood is bare.

Always allow the primer to dry thoroughly before attempting any further work on the piece. Acrylic primer usually only takes an hour to dry. Once fully dry, use fine sandpaper to get the surface smooth, ready for the top coat of paint.

If you plan to use enamel paints (such as Humbrol) for the colour coat, make sure you use acrylic primer rather than an oil-based alternative. The oil-based version of the primer can react with the drying agents in the enamel paint, lengthening the drying time from a couple of hours to several days or more.

Wood stains and varnishes

Wood stains and varnishes can be applied to all natural woods by following the manufacturer's instructions.

MDF needs a special mention as it acts like a sponge, soaking up most solutions; wood stains and varnishes are no exception. If you want to stain MDF, it is best to apply the stain and let it dry completely. If you want to increase the depth of colour, apply a further coat and then let this dry. Once you are satisfied with the colour, apply the varnish as a separate coat on top.

Safety note

If you are making a project to be used by children, make sure that the finish you apply is one of the non-toxic varieties. This information is always carried on the container.

See also 'Safety' section on page 4.

A range of enamel paints

Projects

See Teleidoscope project on page 102

Egg timer

This egg timer is a popular and useful project for the kitchen.

Although egg-timer glasses are usually of standard dimensions, check yours against the dimensions given and, if necessary, adjust them as appropriate.

The top and bottom retaining caps are glued to the uprights and give a 'mirror image' pattern, so that the egg timer will look the same whichever way up it happens to be.

It is best to use rapid-setting epoxy resin for the gluing operation, as this will eliminate any chance of components 'creeping' while the glue is setting.

The completed timer ready for duty in the kitchen

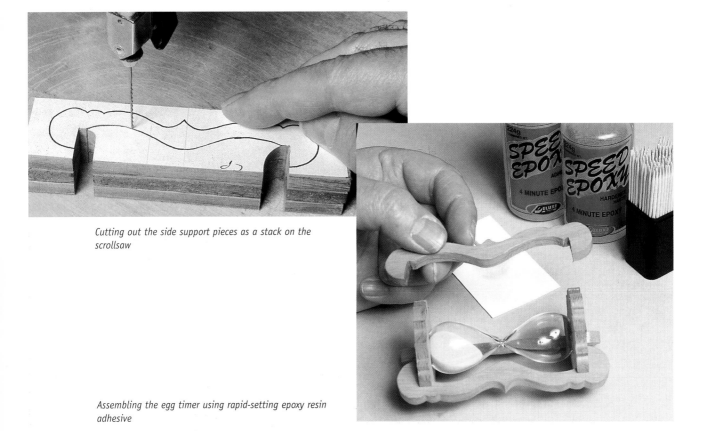

Cutting out the side support pieces as a stack on the scrollsaw

Assembling the egg timer using rapid-setting epoxy resin adhesive

10

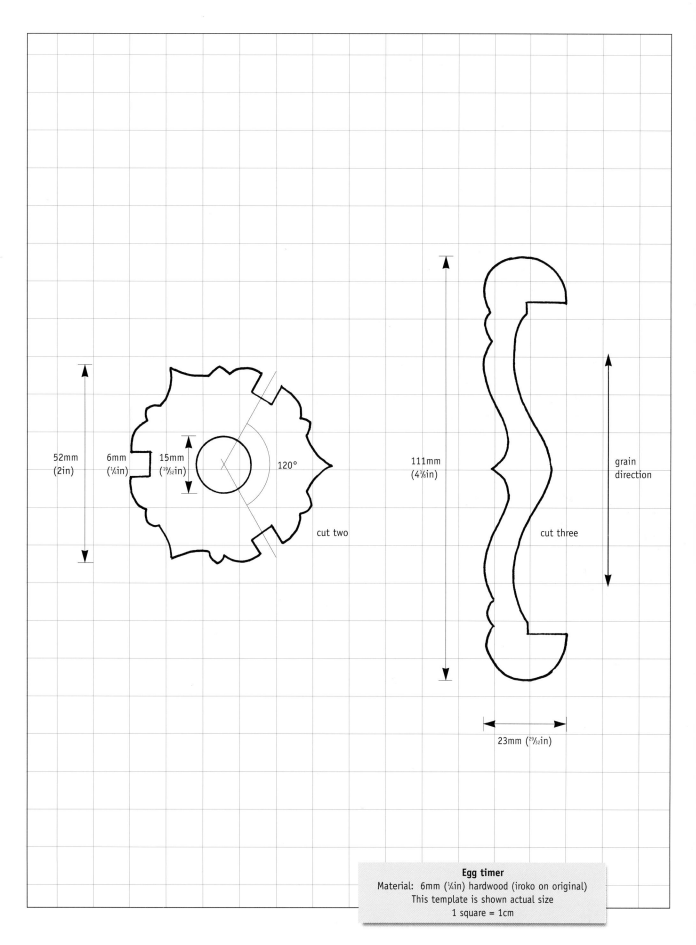

52mm
(2in)

6mm
(¼in)

15mm
(¹⁹⁄₃₂in)

120°

cut two

111mm
(4⅜in)

grain
direction

cut three

23mm (²⁹⁄₃₂in)

Egg timer
Material: 6mm (¼in) hardwood (iroko on original)
This template is shown actual size
1 square = 1cm

Sauce bottle holder

This makes a neat holder for the ketchup and brown sauce so loved by youngsters, and serves the useful purpose of keeping the containers both upright and tidy on the dining table.

The top panel has cutouts for the actual sauce containers, which can be modified to suit the size of the containers you want to use with the holder. The 'bottles' used here are the standard squeezy type, available from most kitchen suppliers.

Cut out all the parts, and paint them in your chosen colours before assembly.

To assemble, first glue the two halves of

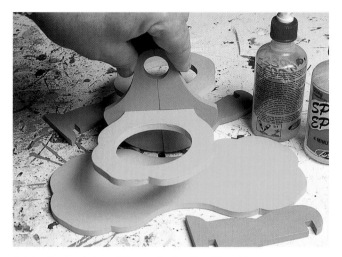

Joining the two halves of the carrying handle with rapid-setting adhesive

the carrier to the top panel of the holder, using rapid-setting epoxy resin adhesive. Join the top and bottom panels in the same way, and your sauce bottle holder is complete and ready for use.

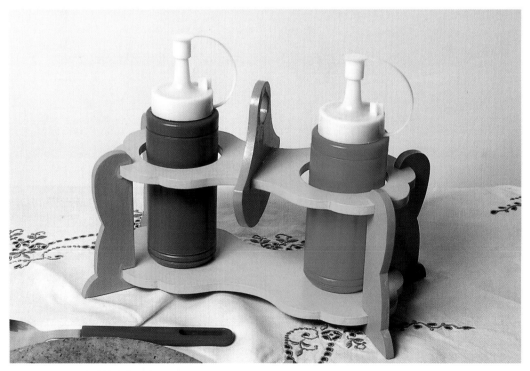

The completed sauce bottle holder ready for use

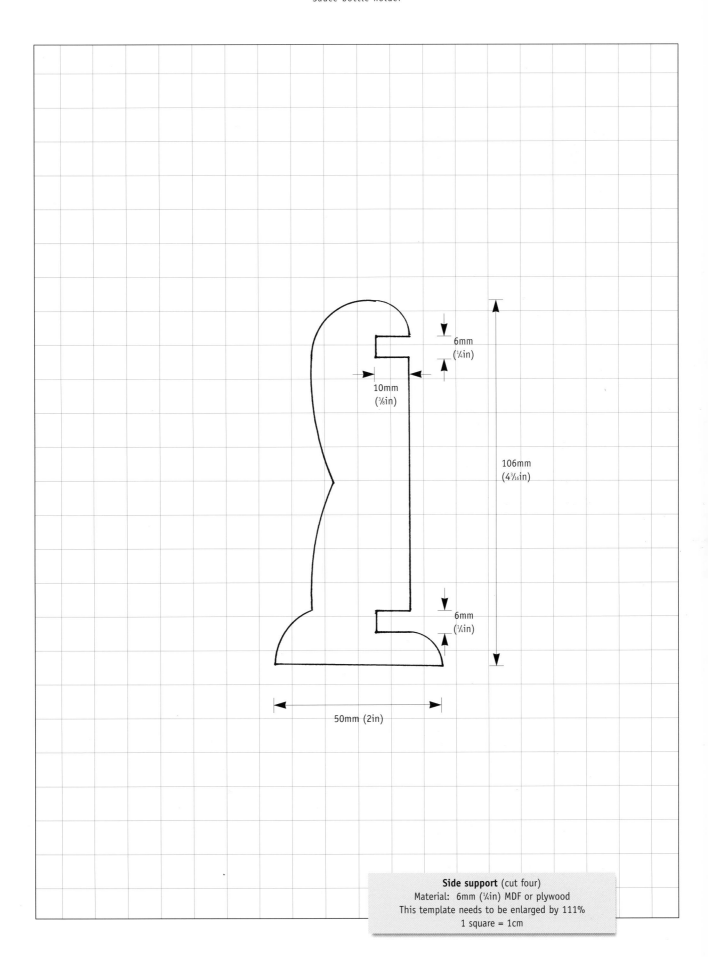

6mm
(¼in)

10mm
(⅜in)

106mm
(4³⁄₁₆in)

6mm
(¼in)

50mm (2in)

Side support (cut four)
Material: 6mm (¼in) MDF or plywood
This template needs to be enlarged by 111%
1 square = 1cm

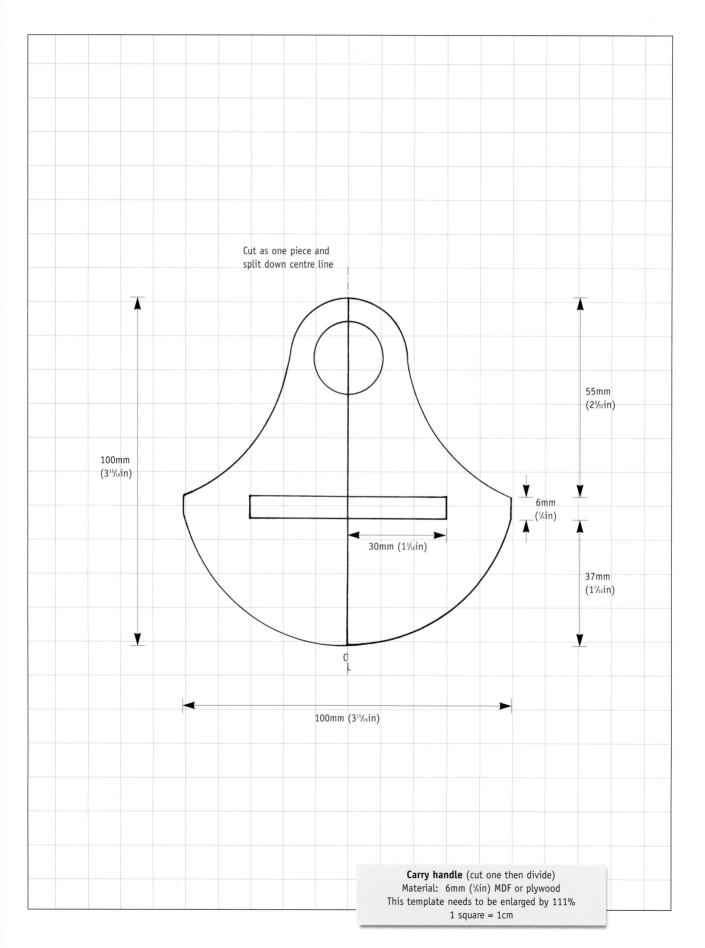

Cut as one piece and
split down centre line

55mm
(2⁹⁄₃₂in)

100mm
(3¹⁵⁄₁₆in)

6mm
(¼in)

30mm (1³⁄₁₆in)

37mm
(1⁷⁄₁₆in)

100mm (3¹⁵⁄₁₆in)

Carry handle (cut one then divide)
Material: 6mm (¼in) MDF or plywood
This template needs to be enlarged by 111%
1 square = 1cm

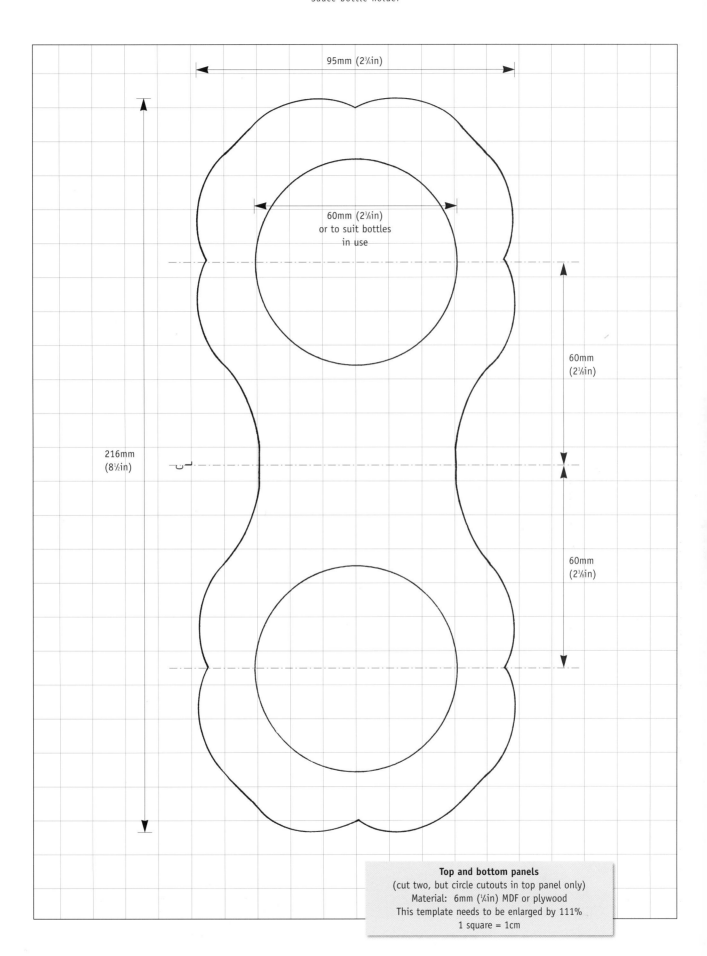

95mm (2¾in)

60mm (2⅜in)
or to suit bottles
in use

216mm
(8½in)

C L

60mm
(2⅜in)

60mm
(2⅜in)

Top and bottom panels
(cut two, but circle cutouts in top panel only)
Material: 6mm (¼in) MDF or plywood
This template needs to be enlarged by 111%
1 square = 1cm

Memo board with clock

This kitchen memo board is invaluable as a shopping list and for noting appointments, and it has a built-in clock inserted as a useful extra.

The interior of the memo board is bevel cut from its surround with a fine blade, and painted separately. When dry, it is glued back in place, so that it is recessed into the surround, which gives a neat finish to the whole piece.

The fixings, which are attached to the back of the memo board, can be either picture rings and wire – as used here – or keyhole plates, which will need two screws.

Make a cutout to fit the size of your chosen clock insert – this is usually about 65mm (2½in). To ensure a secure fit, cut to the inside of your cutting line on the template and then file gently, as necessary, after cutting is complete.

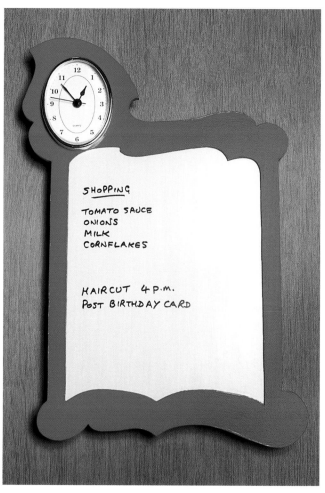

The completed memo board with its clock fitted and running

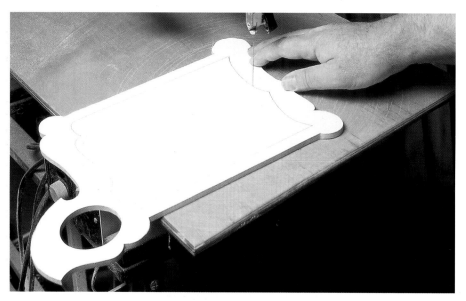

Bevel cutting out the interior of the memo board

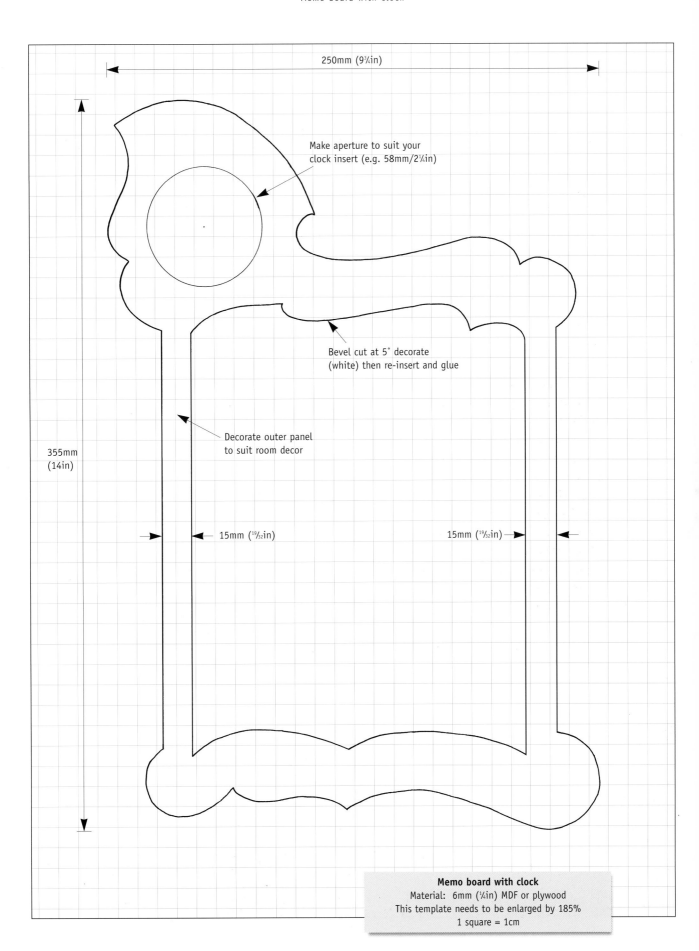

250mm (9¾in)

Make aperture to suit your
clock insert (e.g. 58mm/2¼in)

Bevel cut at 5° decorate
(white) then re-insert and glue

Decorate outer panel
to suit room decor

355mm
(14in)

15mm (¹⁹⁄₃₂in)

15mm (¹⁹⁄₃₂in)

Memo board with clock
Material: 6mm (¼in) MDF or plywood
This template needs to be enlarged by 185%
1 square = 1cm

Shelf with acanthus leaf pattern

This decorative shelf is made from 6mm (¼in) MDF – it leaves a good surface finish, and little work is necessary after cutting out has been completed – but other materials will work just as well and may be preferred.

There are no internal cutouts and two or more shelves can be quite easily cut simultaneously as a stack, if you need to make several shelves.

A mini drill with a small drill bit in place will prove very useful for making pilot holes to fix the shelf and its support bracket. Take care to make the holes vertical, so that the screws enter at right angles, as this will ensure that the shelf and its bracket are kept straight in

The finished shelf

the completed piece.

Add a smear of wood glue to the back of the shelf and to the top and rear surfaces of the support bracket when assembling.

Cutting around the more intricate parts of the main shelf panel

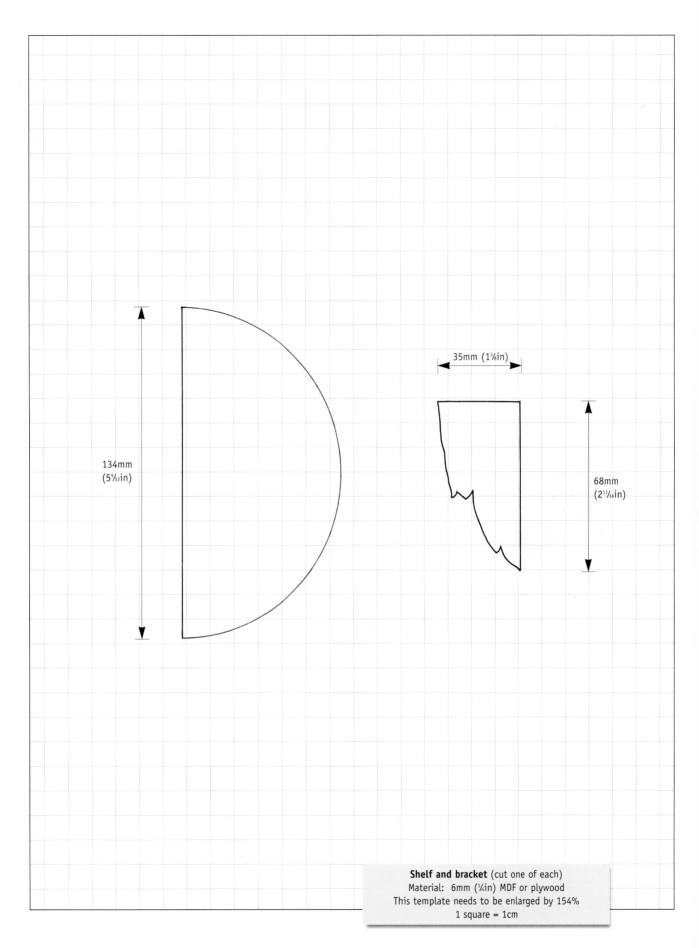

134mm
(5⁹/₃₂in)

35mm (1⅜in)

68mm
(2¹¹/₁₆in)

Shelf and bracket (cut one of each)
Material: 6mm (¼in) MDF or plywood
This template needs to be enlarged by 154%
1 square = 1cm

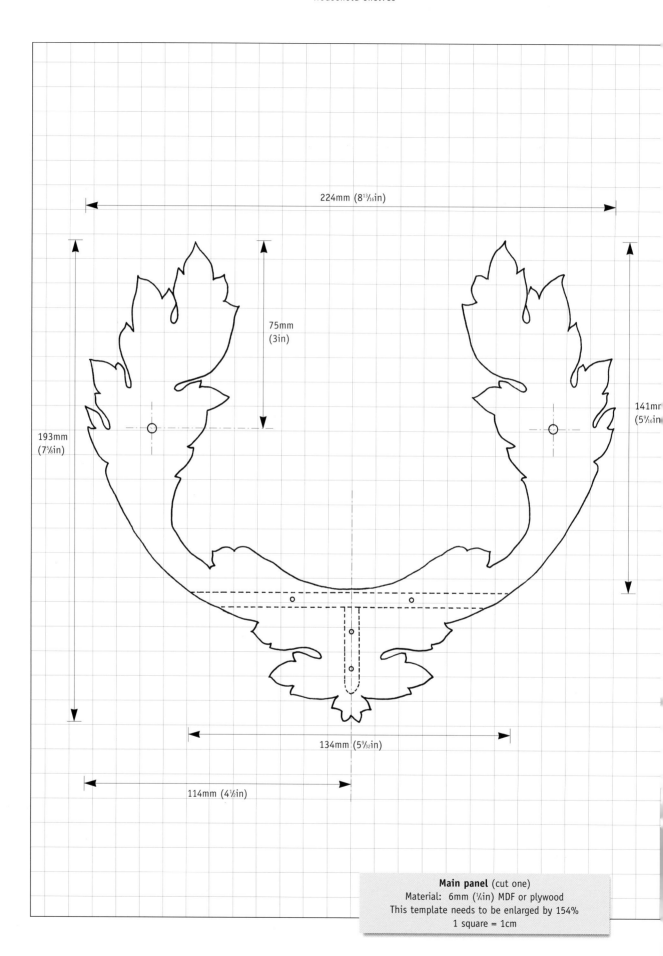

224mm (8¹³⁄₁₆in)

75mm
(3in)

141mm
(5⁹⁄₁₆in)

193mm
(7⅝in)

134mm (5⁹⁄₃₂in)

114mm (4½in)

Main panel (cut one)
Material: 6mm (¼in) MDF or plywood
This template needs to be enlarged by 154%
1 square = 1cm

Art Nouveau-style shelf

This simple but elegant scroll shelf is inspired by the Art Nouveau style. It can be made easily and economically using 6mm (¼in) MDF.

Choose paint colours to either match or contrast with your existing room decor, and decorate the individual components of the shelf prior to assembly to ensure a good sharp paint line where the two colours meet.

The shelf has been decorated and fitted, and the support bracket can now be marked accurately

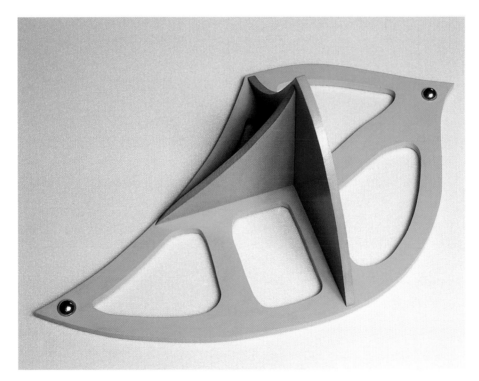

The completed shelf ready to hang up

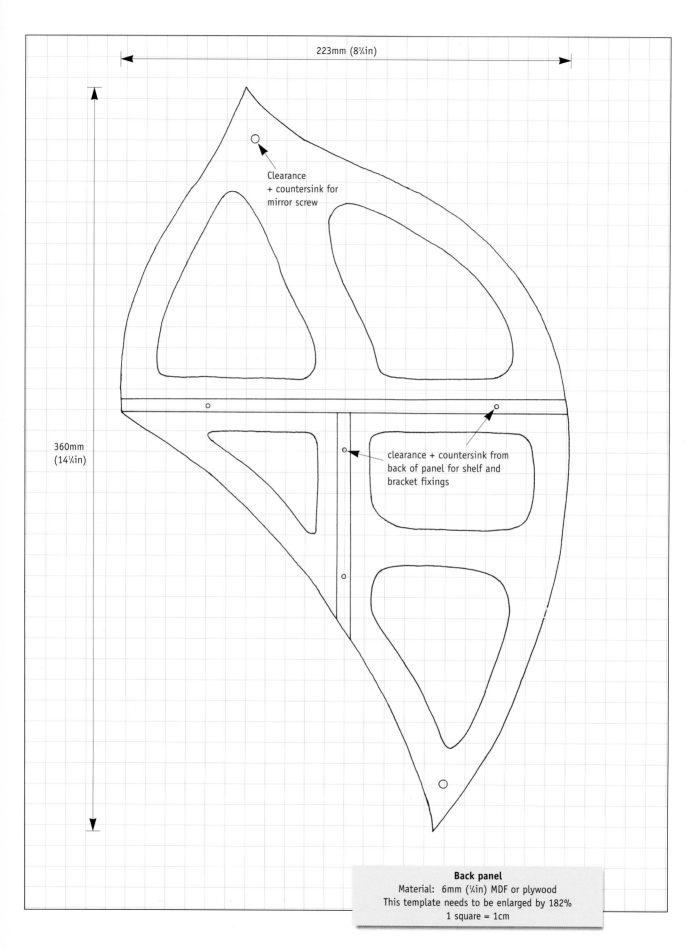

223mm (8¾in)

360mm
(14¼in)

Clearance
+ countersink for
mirror screw

clearance + countersink from
back of panel for shelf and
bracket fixings

Back panel
Material: 6mm (¼in) MDF or plywood
This template needs to be enlarged by 182%
1 square = 1cm

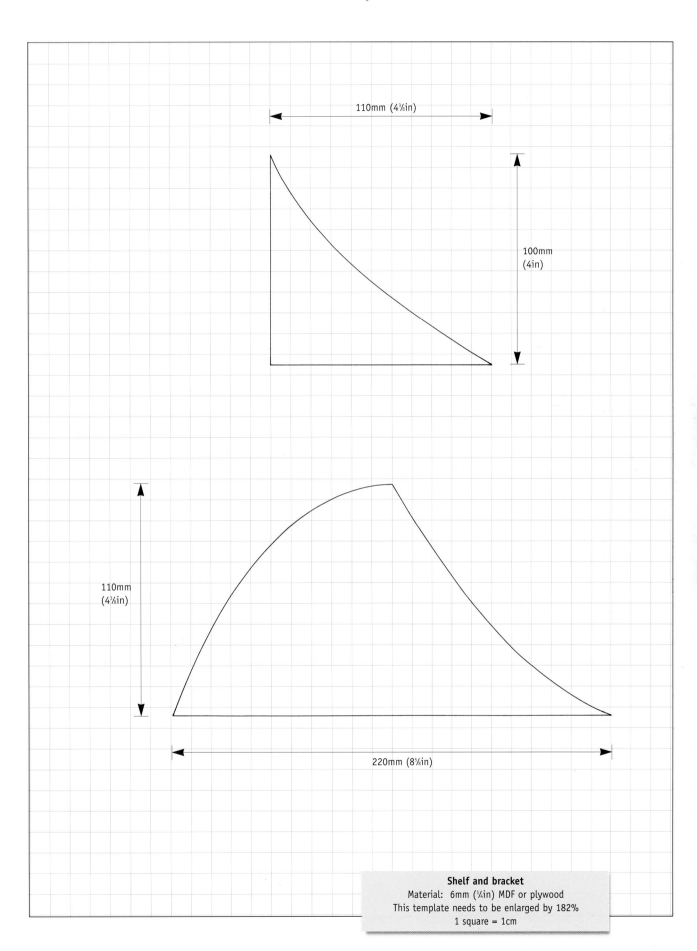

110mm (4⅜in)

100mm
(4in)

110mm
(4⅜in)

220mm (8⅝in)

Shelf and bracket
Material: 6mm (¼in) MDF or plywood
This template needs to be enlarged by 182%
1 square = 1cm

Complementary
pair of shelves
(positive and negative)

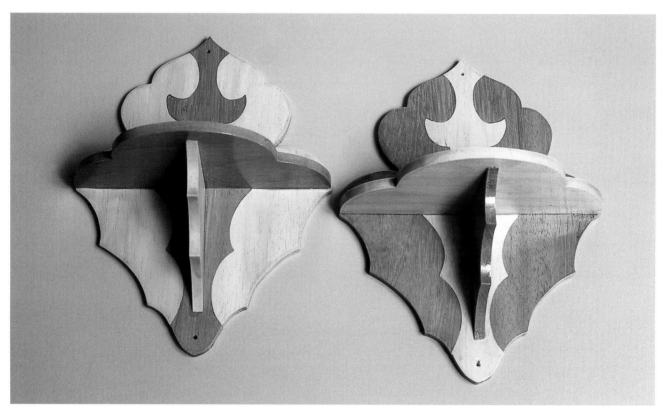

The completed pair of complementary shelves

The shelves shown here are made from obeche (light-coloured wood) and iroko (dark-coloured wood) but, if your prefer, you could choose two different varieties of contrasting wood.

If possible, select woods of the same thickness but, if they do vary, sand the surface of one to match the other. Cut the two woods out as a stack, and you will then have all the wood that you need to make up this pair of positive and negative shelves.

To guard against movement when cutting out the shapes, first join the two woods together with small brass panel pins (stronger than adhesive), then place the cutting pattern on the wood sandwich. Once the parts are cut, clean up any saw tearout with fine sandpaper before assembly.

Make up the back panels first. The curved design in the centre section helps to hold the components together, but adhesive is of course

The cutting pattern in place on the wood 'sandwich'. Note the small brass panel pins holding the sandwich together

required as well. Glue the parts together, and leave until the adhesive is thoroughly set.

Next, mark out the pilot holes for the shelf and bracket fixing. It is easiest and most accurate to fit the shelf first and then offer up the bracket to mark out the pilot holes for its fixing screws.

If attractive woods are used to construct these shelves, a polish is all that is needed to decorate them. If you prefer to paint the shelves, you can make them up in MDF or ply, and still retain the positive/negative effect by painting them prior to assembly with a suitable colour scheme.

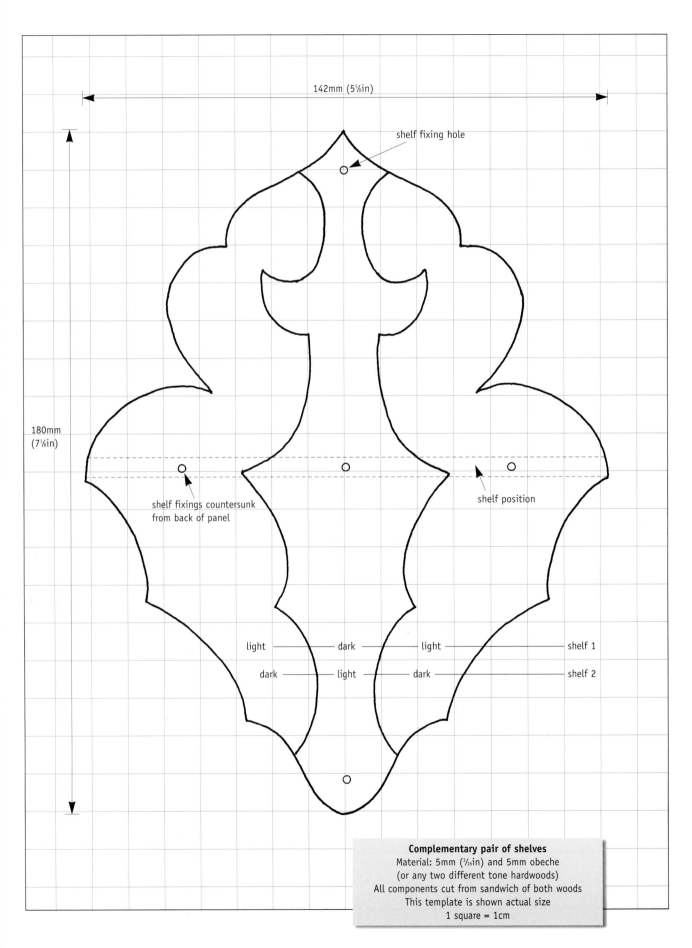

142mm (5⅝in)

180mm
(7⅛in)

shelf fixing hole

shelf fixings countersunk
from back of panel

shelf position

| light | dark | light | shelf 1 |
| dark | light | dark | shelf 2 |

Complementary pair of shelves
Material: 5mm (³⁄₁₆in) and 5mm obeche
(or any two different tone hardwoods)
All components cut from sandwich of both woods
This template is shown actual size
1 square = 1cm

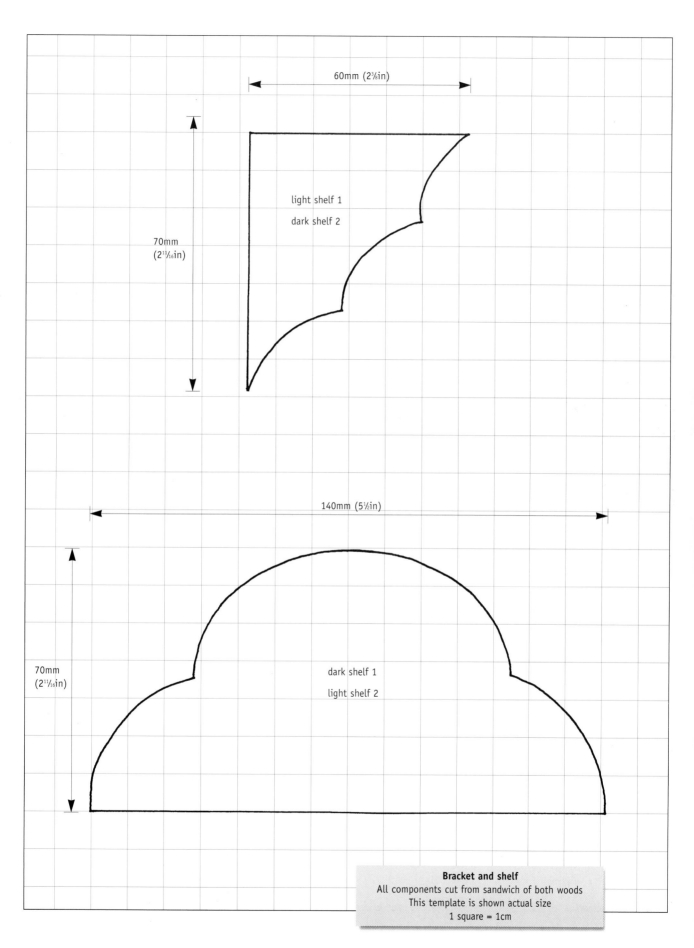

60mm (2⅜in)

70mm
(2¹¹⁄₁₆in)

light shelf 1

dark shelf 2

140mm (5½in)

70mm
(2¹¹⁄₁₆in)

dark shelf 1

light shelf 2

Bracket and shelf
All components cut from sandwich of both woods
This template is shown actual size
1 square = 1cm

Key rack

The finished key rack, varnished to prevent the mild steel from rusting

The example shown here was made from an offcut of 3mm (⅛in) steel sheet, brushed over with wire wool to give it a satin finish. Brass-plated cup hooks were used for the key holders. As the material used was thin, the surplus thread had to be cut off the cup hooks, to prevent them protruding through the back of the piece, and the threaded portion needed to be reinforced with epoxy resin adhesive. To complete the 'metallic' look of the piece, the completed item was fixed in position using mirror screws with dome caps.

You could, of course, use another material for this key rack and, if the chosen material is sufficiently thick, you will not need to modify the length of the cup hook screw heads.

The panel for the key rack, cut from an offcut of steel sheet

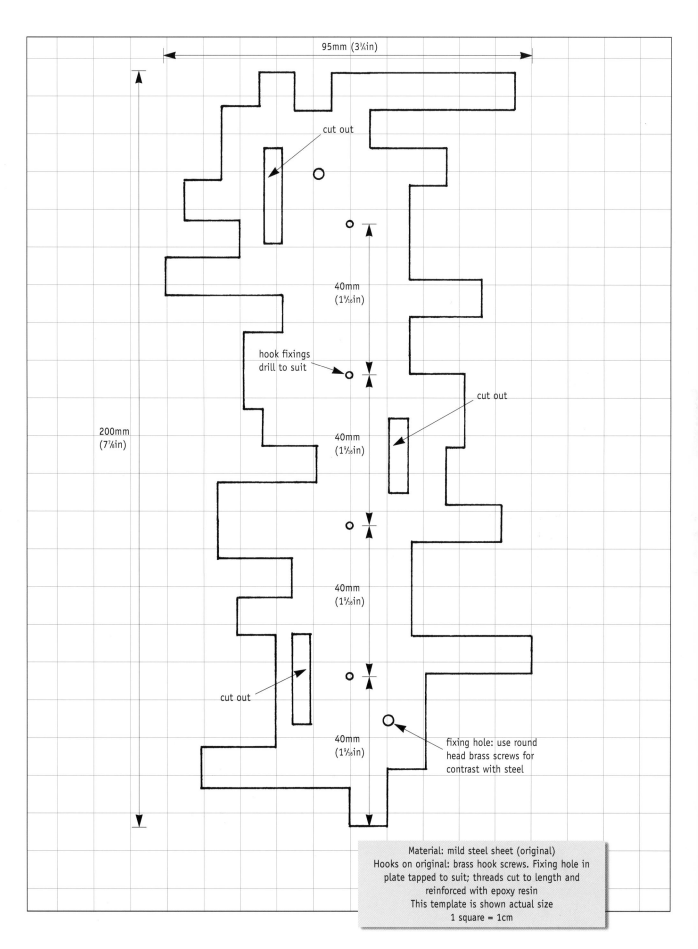

95mm (3¾in)

cut out

200mm
(7⅞in)

40mm
(1⅝in)

hook fixings
drill to suit

cut out

40mm
(1⅝in)

40mm
(1⅝in)

cut out

40mm
(1⅝in)

fixing hole: use round
head brass screws for
contrast with steel

Material: mild steel sheet (original)
Hooks on original: brass hook screws. Fixing hole in
plate tapped to suit; threads cut to length and
reinforced with epoxy resin
This template is shown actual size
1 square = 1cm

Coat rack

This design is simple to cut out and can be lengthened if required to accommodate more hangers. The fixing screws are actually hidden beneath the brass coat hooks so that no fixings show once the rack is in its place. This means that the two end coat hooks are finally screwed down after the rack has been fixed in position on the wall.

The edges of the design have been bevel cut, to make the most of the end grain showing on the cutouts, but cut them vertically if you prefer.

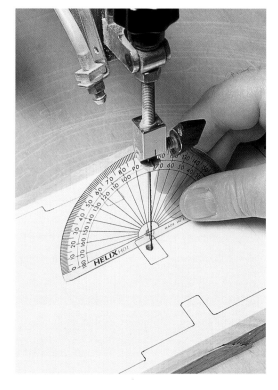

Using a protractor to check the angle of the scrollsaw blade before making the bevel cuts around the coat rack

The completed project with no fixing screws showing

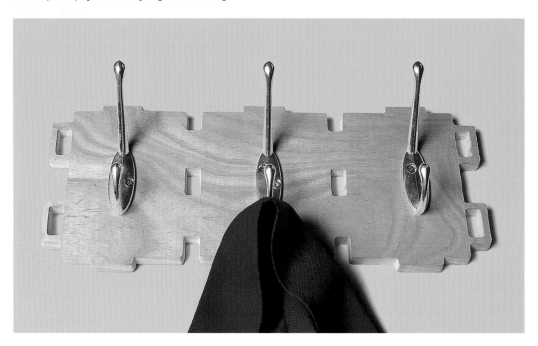

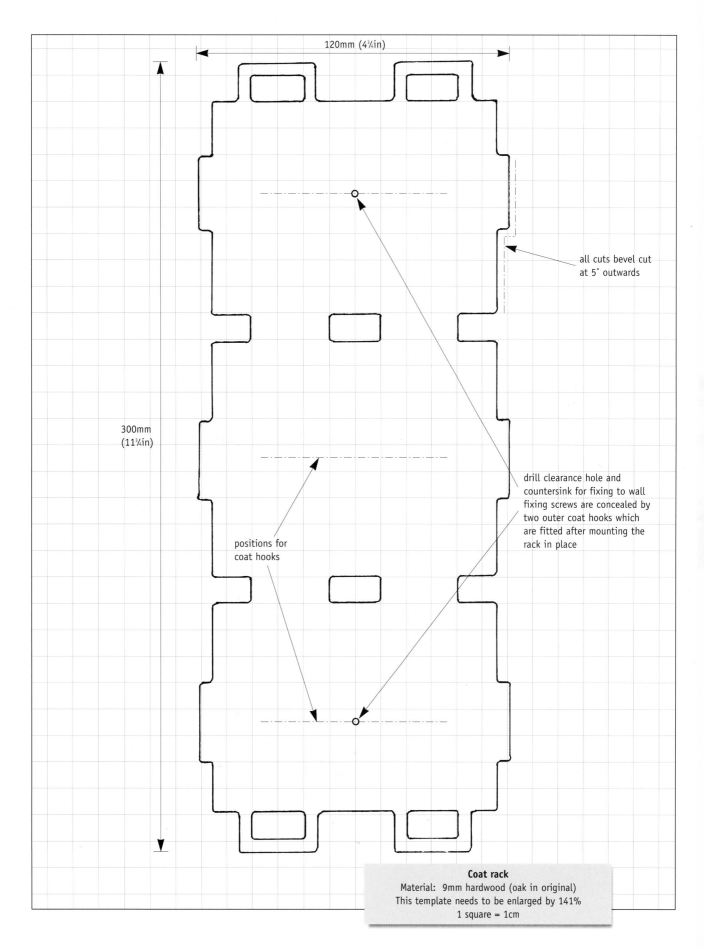

120mm (4¾in)

300mm
(11¾in)

all cuts bevel cut
at 5° outwards

drill clearance hole and
countersink for fixing to wall
fixing screws are concealed by
two outer coat hooks which
are fitted after mounting the
rack in place

positions for
coat hooks

Coat rack
Material: 9mm hardwood (oak in original)
This template needs to be enlarged by 141%
1 square = 1cm

Desk tidy

Although this item is functional, and keeps pens, pencils, paper clips etc under control, the decoration is purely fun and intended to inject a smile into the day in the office. Use whatever colours you prefer for the finish.

Once all the parts are cut out, use corner cramps, if you have them, to assemble the sides, back and front and to keep everything square. To assemble, glue and then pin the components. I used brass panel pins on the one shown here – they won't show, as the unit is painted after construction is complete.

When you have assembled the unit, paint the background colours and, while they are drying, decorate the overlay items. Once the background paint is thoroughly dry, attach the overlays with a little glue. Rapid-setting epoxy resin adhesive was used for the one shown.

The completed desk tidy

Assembling the framework using corner cramps

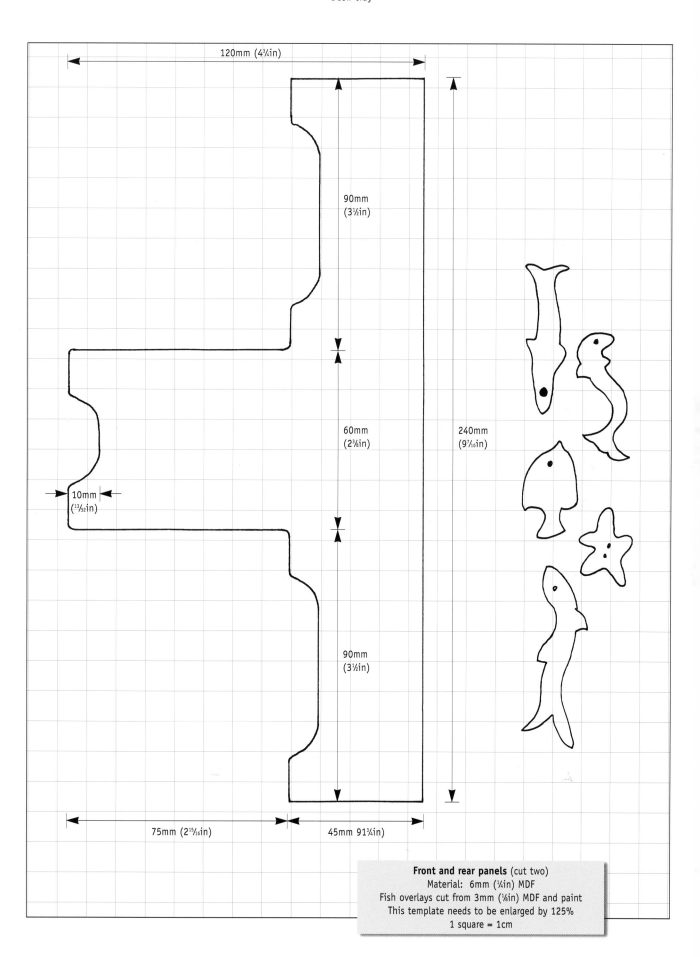

120mm (4¾in)

90mm
(3½in)

60mm
(2⅜in)

240mm
(9⁷⁄₁₆in)

10mm
(¹³⁄₃₂in)

90mm
(3½in)

75mm (2¹⁵⁄₁₆in)

45mm 91¾in)

Front and rear panels (cut two)
Material: 6mm (¼in) MDF
Fish overlays cut from 3mm (⅛in) MDF and paint
This template needs to be enlarged by 125%
1 square = 1cm

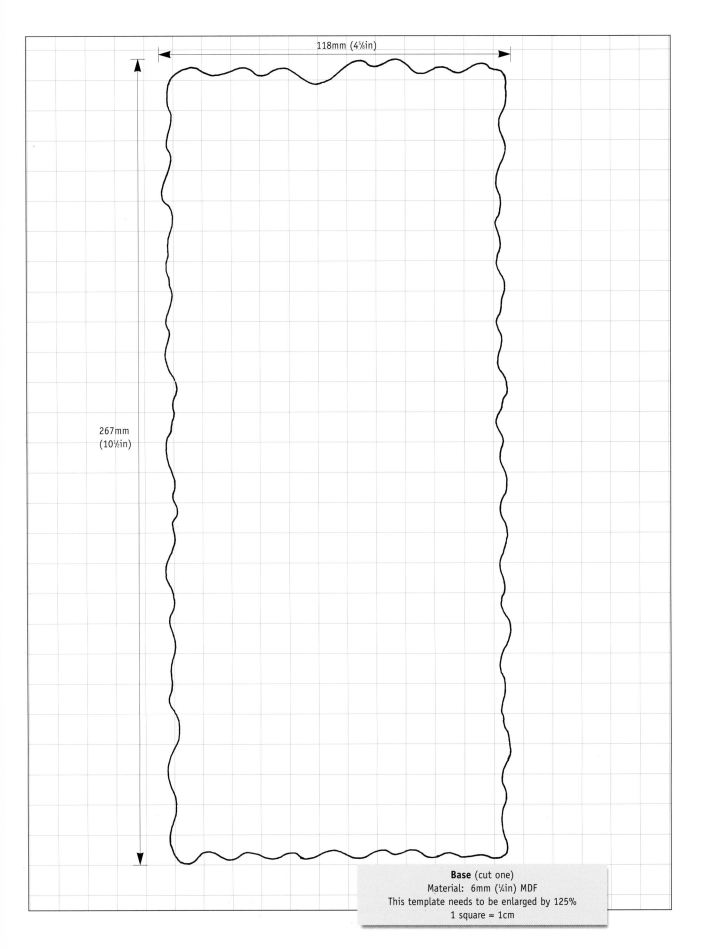

118mm (4⅝in)

267mm
(10½in)

Base (cut one)
Material: 6mm (¼in) MDF
This template needs to be enlarged by 125%
1 square = 1cm

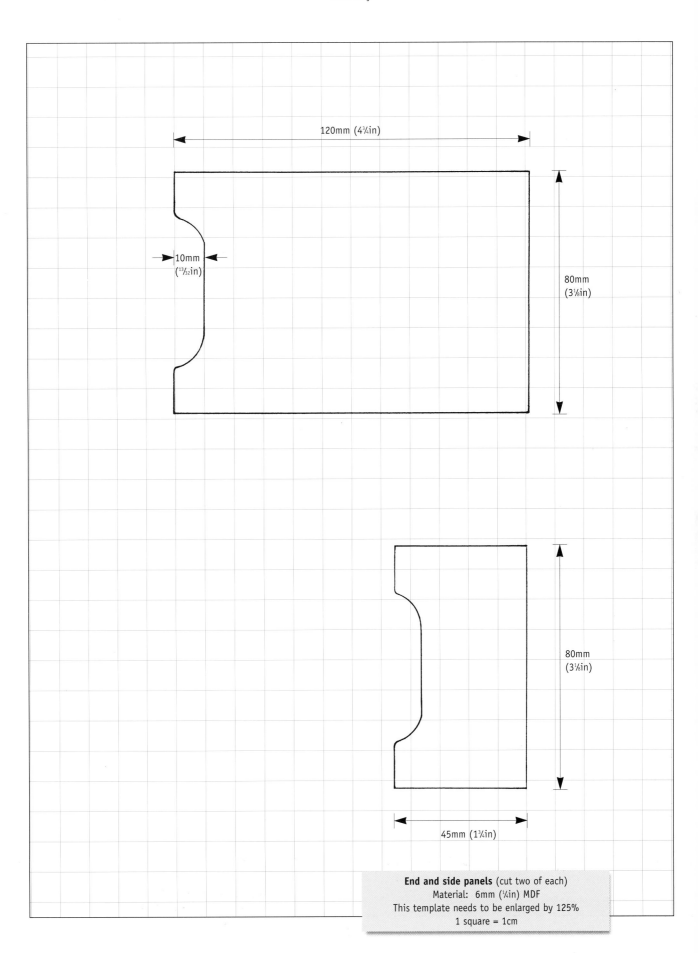

120mm (4¾in)

10mm
(¹³⁄₃₂in)

80mm
(3⅛in)

80mm
(3⅛in)

45mm (1¾in)

End and side panels (cut two of each)
Material: 6mm (¼in) MDF
This template needs to be enlarged by 125%
1 square = 1cm

Trellis panel

This attractive trellis panel measures 1.11 x
0.61m (4 x 2ft) but, if you use a spiral
scrollsaw blade, it can be cut on a small
scrollsaw, as a throat depth of 36.5cm (12in)
is sufficient to reach the centre of the panel.
As the trellis is made from 6mm (¼in) ply,
two panels can be cut at a time, and the
components will still not be too heavy to
manoeuvre.

It is important to support the portion of
ply sheet overhanging the edge of the saw
table, as the leverage on such a large,
unsupported, workpiece could easily snap the
blade. A standard Workmate was used here,
with an offcut of ply held in the jaws to sit at
the same height as the saw table (see
photograph).

For garden use, the finished trellis should
be weatherproofed with an outdoor grade
colour/preservative.

The trellis installed in the garden

*A Workmate being used to
support the large sheet of
ply at the same level as the
saw table to allow cutting
without putting strain on
the blade*

Trellis panel

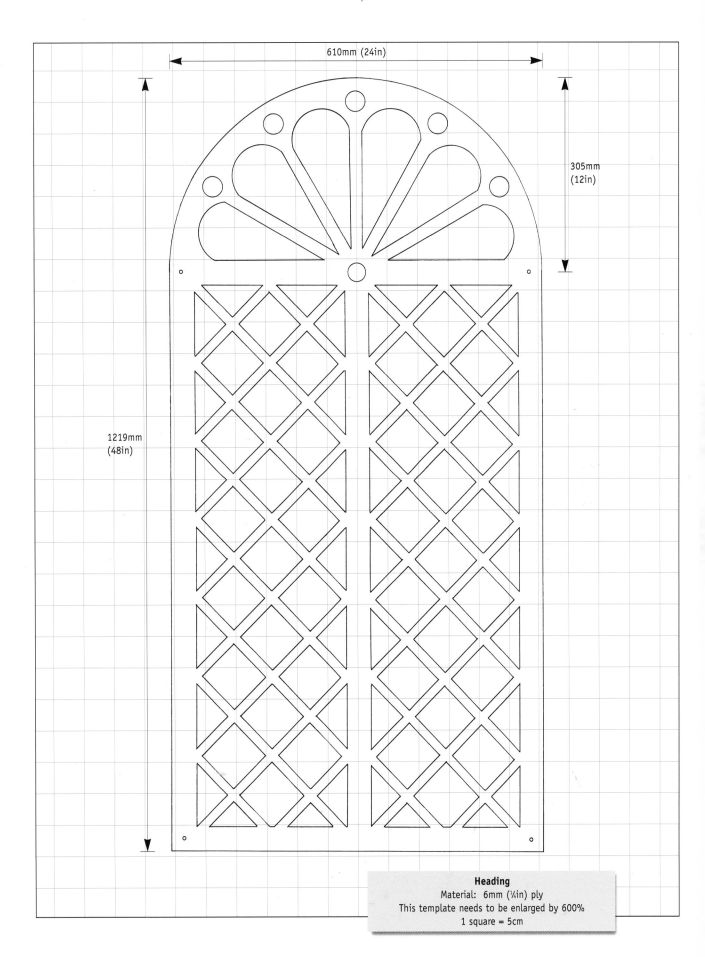

610mm (24in)

305mm
(12in)

1219mm
(48in)

Heading
Material: 6mm (¼in) ply
This template needs to be enlarged by 600%
1 square = 5cm

37

Garden tote

This scrollsaw version of the traditional garden trug is a useful item for any keen gardener. The joints on the bottom panels are scrollcut, and slot in place on the side panels of the tote. No glue is used, as the whole thing is held together by woodscrews in the dowels, which act as spacers and as additional support for the bottom panels.

Cutting out of the panels is straightforward. To assemble, it is best to screw the dowels in place on one of the side panels first, and then to locate the bottom panels in their respective slots in the side panel. Finally, add the remaining side panel and drive home the screws. To decorate the tote, use a garden wood stain/colourant which is totally weatherproof.

The finished project in the garden

Test assembly of the base parts with their supporting/spacing dowels fitted to one side panel. Necessary adjustments can be made at this stage without any difficulty

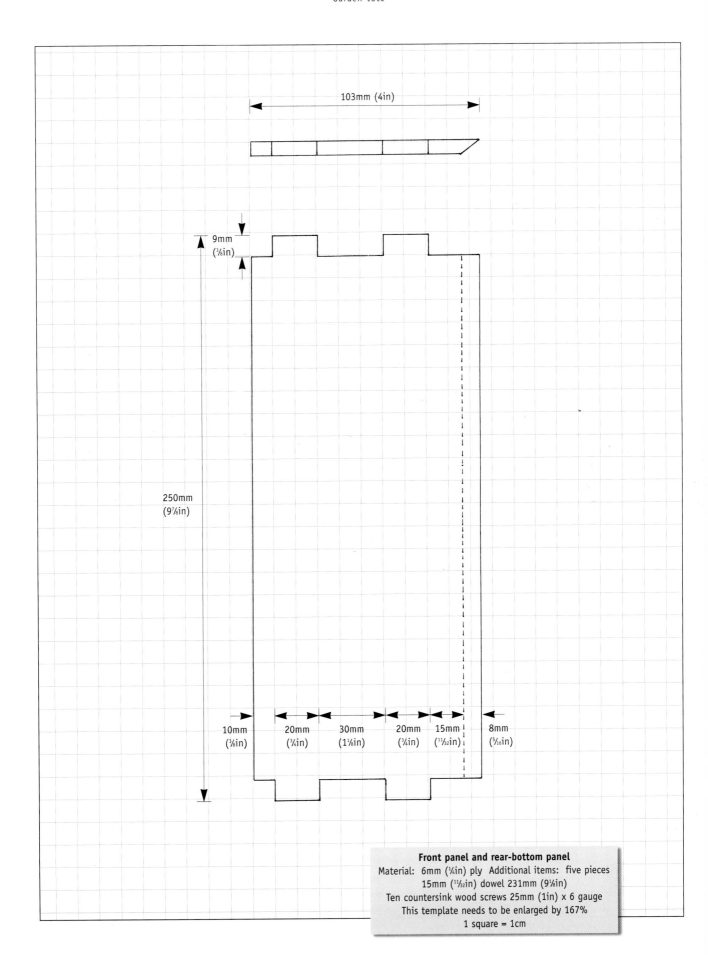

103mm (4in)

9mm
(⅜in)

250mm
(9⅞in)

10mm
(⅜in)

20mm
(¾in)

30mm
(1⅛in)

20mm
(¾in)

15mm
(¹¹⁄₃₂in)

8mm
(⁵⁄₁₆in)

Front panel and rear-bottom panel
Material: 6mm (¼in) ply Additional items: five pieces
15mm (¹¹⁄₃₂in) dowel 231mm (9⅛in)
Ten countersink wood screws 25mm (1in) x 6 gauge
This template needs to be enlarged by 167%
1 square = 1cm

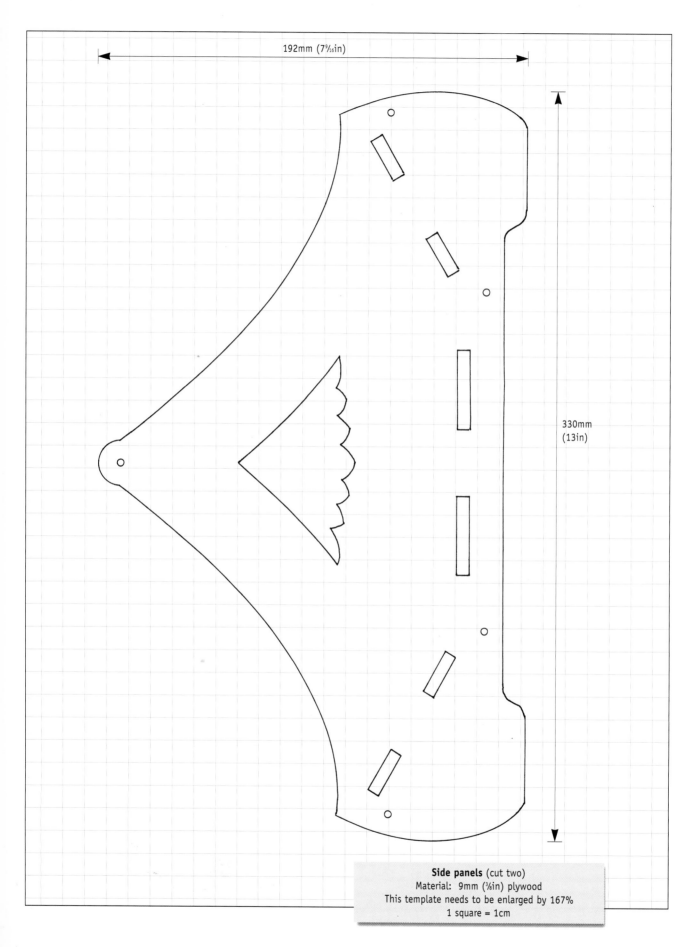

192mm (7⁹⁄₁₆in)

330mm
(13in)

Side panels (cut two)
Material: 9mm (⅜in) plywood
This template needs to be enlarged by 167%
1 square = 1cm

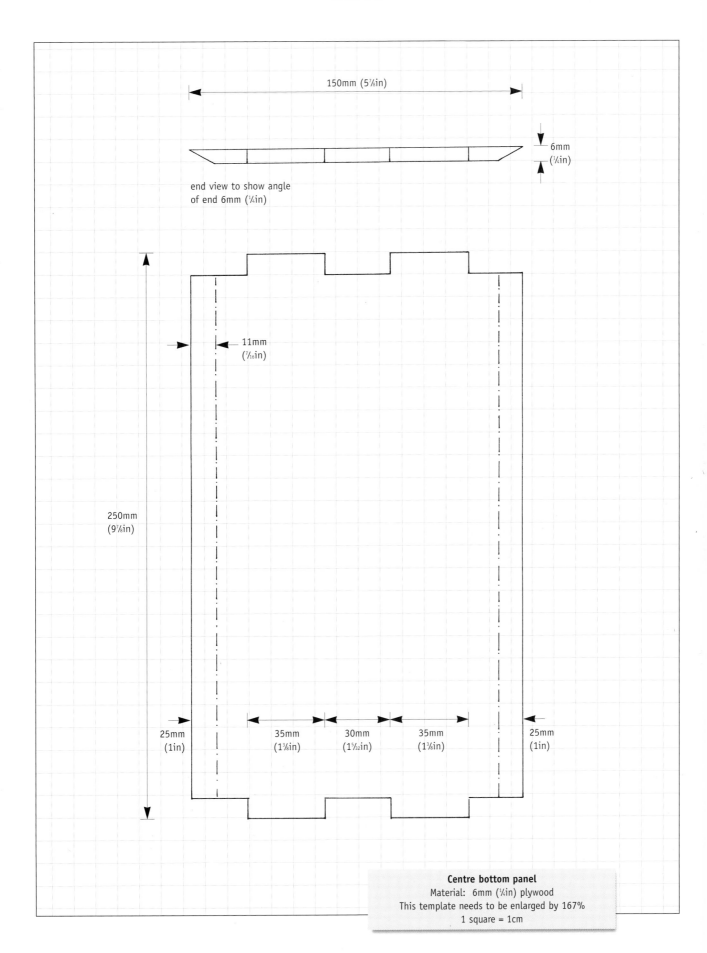

150mm (5⅞in)

6mm
(¼in)

end view to show angle
of end 6mm (¼in)

11mm
(⁷/₁₆in)

250mm
(9⅞in)

25mm
(1in)

35mm
(1⅜in)

30mm
(1⁵/₃₂in)

35mm
(1⅜in)

25mm
(1in)

Centre bottom panel
Material: 6mm (¼in) plywood
This template needs to be enlarged by 167%
1 square = 1cm

Nest box

This straightforward and appealing project can be made entirely from pieces of 6mm (¼in) ply. The basic structure is glued and pinned with small brass pins and then the decorative overlay is added once the basic structure is complete.

The nesting hole and the small hole in the lower decorative overlay provide access to the fixing screws which are drilled through the back panel.

The completed project ready for its tenants

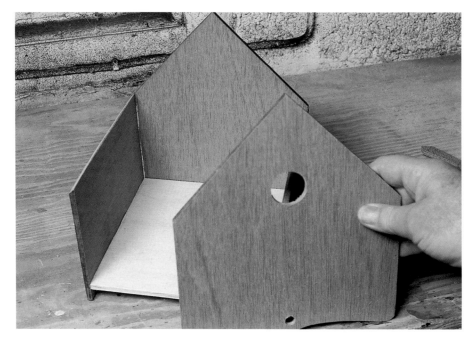

Assembling the basic nest box

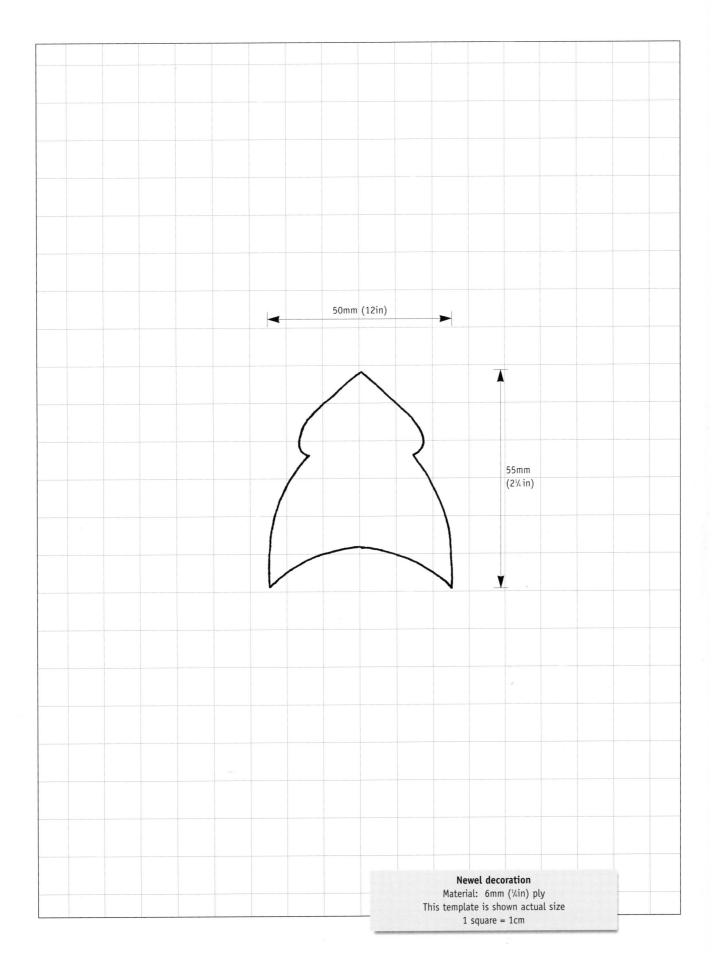

50mm (12in)

55mm
(2¼ in)

Newel decoration
Material: 6mm (¼in) ply
This template is shown actual size
1 square = 1cm

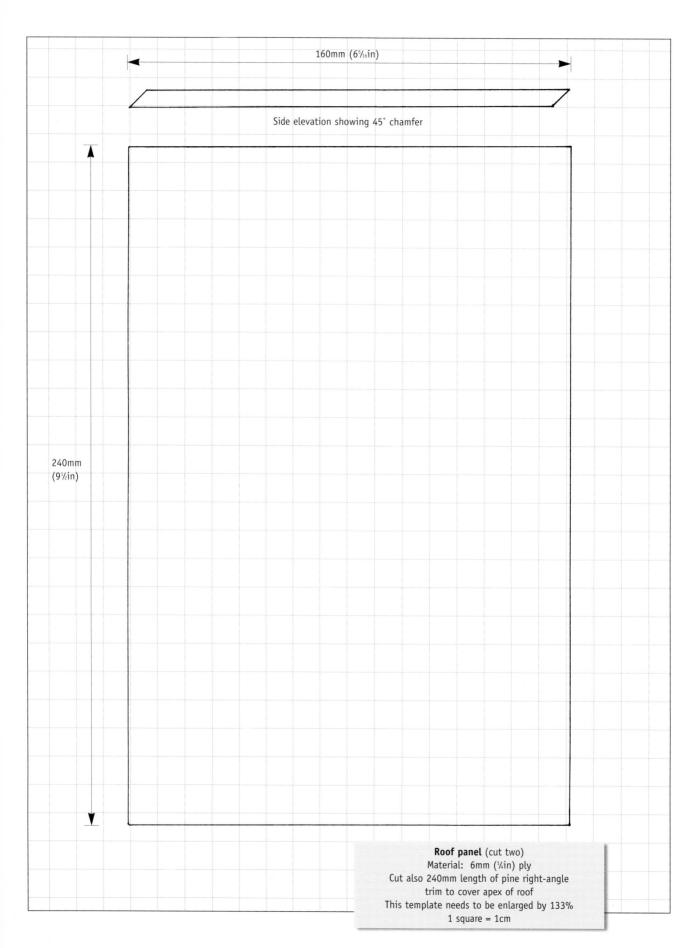

160mm (6⁵⁄₁₆in)

Side elevation showing 45° chamfer

240mm
(9½in)

Roof panel (cut two)
Material: 6mm (¼in) ply
Cut also 240mm length of pine right-angle
trim to cover apex of roof
This template needs to be enlarged by 133%
1 square = 1cm

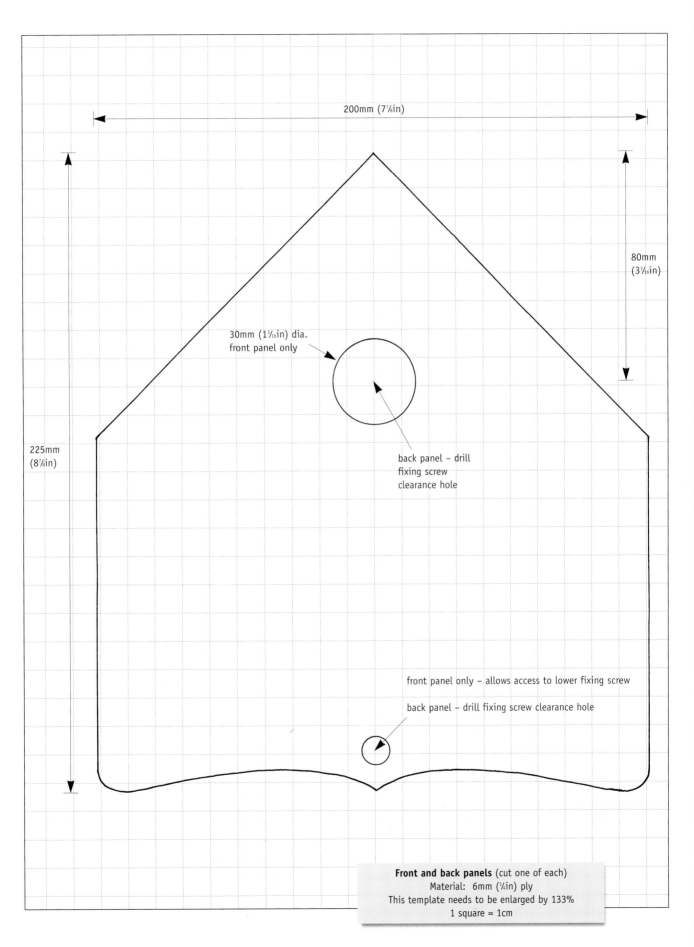

200mm (7⅞in)

80mm (3³⁄₁₆in)

30mm (1³⁄₁₆in) dia.
front panel only

back panel – drill
fixing screw
clearance hole

225mm
(8⅞in)

front panel only – allows access to lower fixing screw

back panel – drill fixing screw clearance hole

Front and back panels (cut one of each)
Material: 6mm (¼in) ply
This template needs to be enlarged by 133%
1 square = 1cm

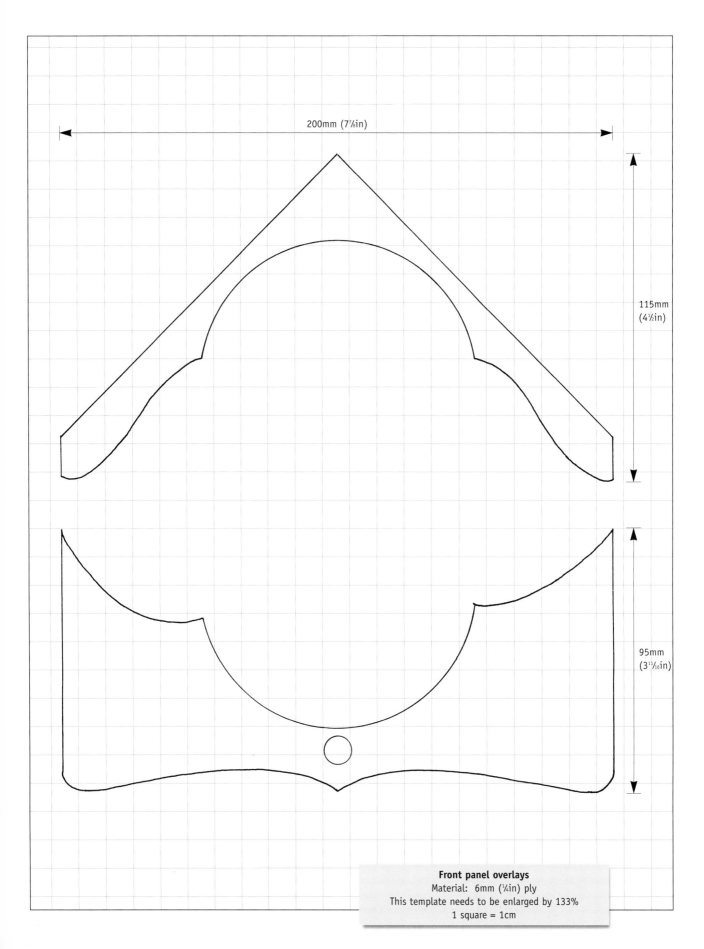

200mm (7⅞in)

115mm (4½in)

95mm (3¹¹⁄₁₆in)

Front panel overlays
Material: 6mm (¼in) ply
This template needs to be enlarged by 133%
1 square = 1cm

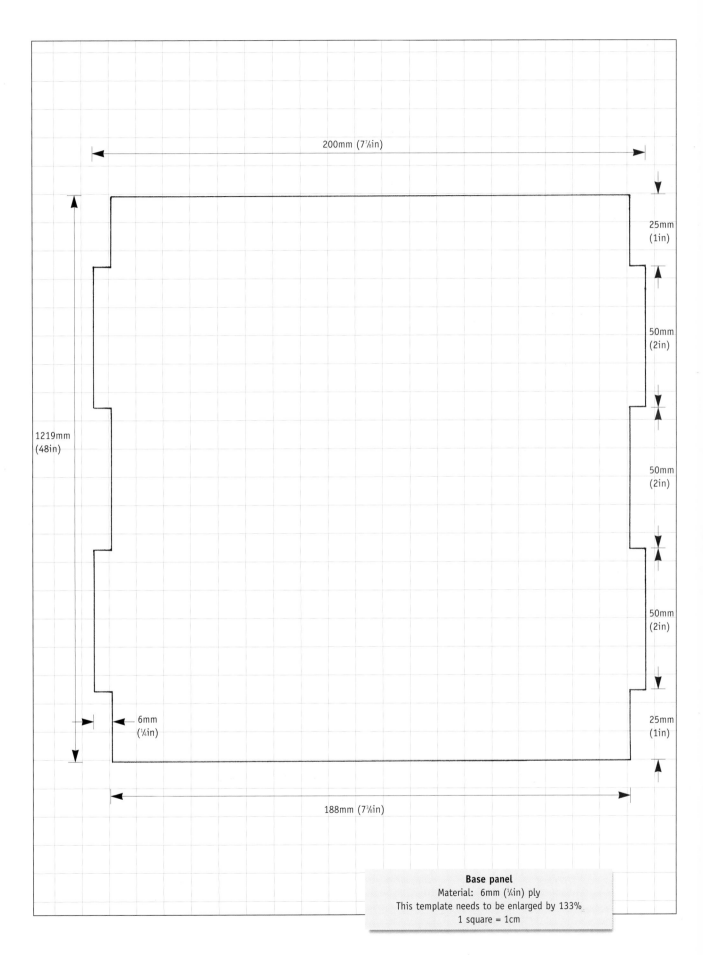

200mm (7⅞in)

25mm
(1in)

50mm
(2in)

50mm
(2in)

1219mm
(48in)

50mm
(2in)

6mm
(¼in)

25mm
(1in)

188mm (7⅜in)

Base panel
Material: 6mm (¼in) ply
This template needs to be enlarged by 133%
1 square = 1cm

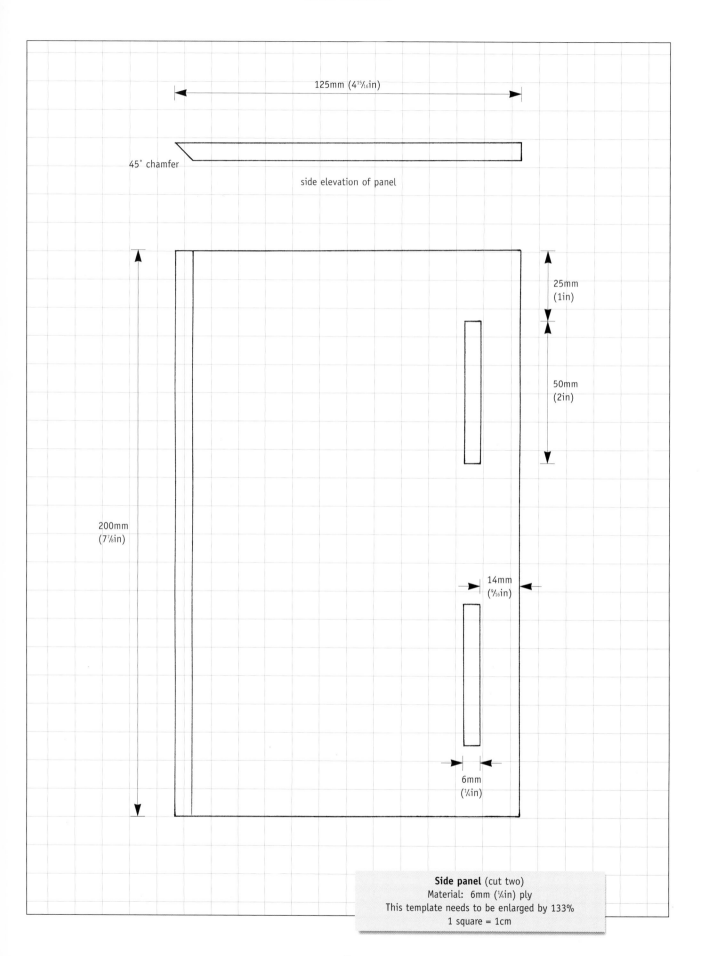

125mm (4¹⁵⁄₁₆in)

45° chamfer

side elevation of panel

25mm (1in)

50mm (2in)

200mm (7⁷⁄₈in)

14mm (⁹⁄₁₆in)

6mm (¼in)

Side panel (cut two)
Material: 6mm (¼in) ply
This template needs to be enlarged by 133%
1 square = 1cm

Garden accessories rack

This little project serves to keep all those loose garden items such as tools, twine and fertilizer bottles in one place and ready for use. The rack has hooks for hanging a trowel, fork and other small garden tools below the shelf.

To attach the rack to a convenient wall, fit keyhole plates on the rear of the back panel – this will give the finished rack a neat finish, as no screw heads will be visible. The peg joints on the end of the shelf give the rack a suitably rustic appearance as well as securing the end panels.

Assembly is easiest if you make up the centre section first. Screw in the hanging hooks and then glue and screw the back panel to the shelf. Make sure the heads of your wood screws will clear the opening in the keyhole plates, then add the side panels.

It is best to decorate the rack with a water-resistant wood stain or colourant, as garden tools can often be put away wet.

The completed rack in use

Fixing the hanging hooks underneath the shelf

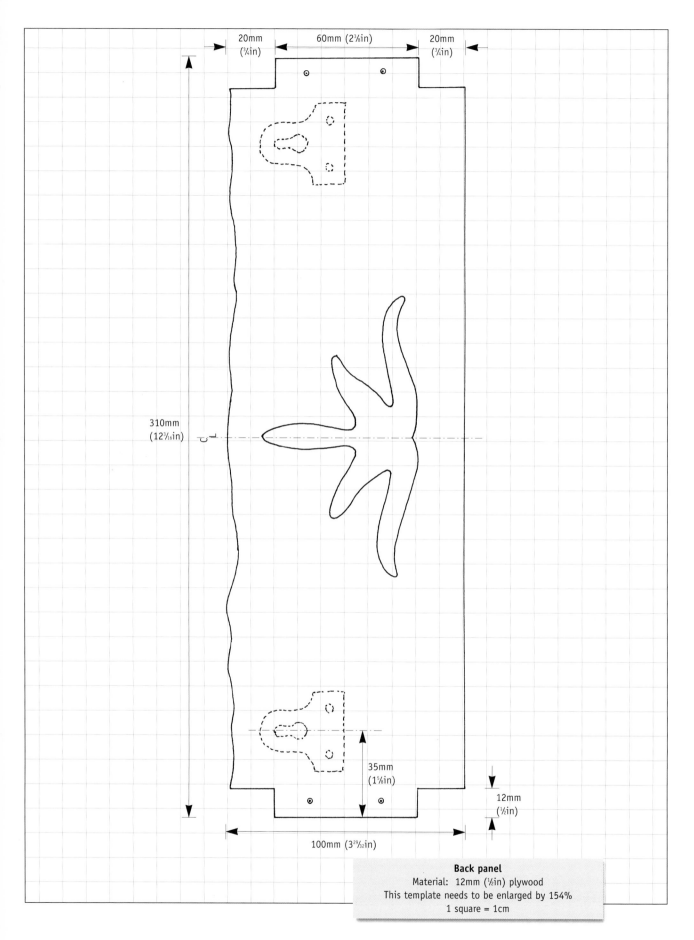

20mm
(³⁄₄in)

60mm (2³⁄₈in)

20mm
(³⁄₄in)

310mm
(12³⁄₁₆in)

C L

35mm
(1⅜in)

12mm
(½in)

100mm (3²⁹⁄₃₂in)

Back panel
Material: 12mm (½in) plywood
This template needs to be enlarged by 154%
1 square = 1cm

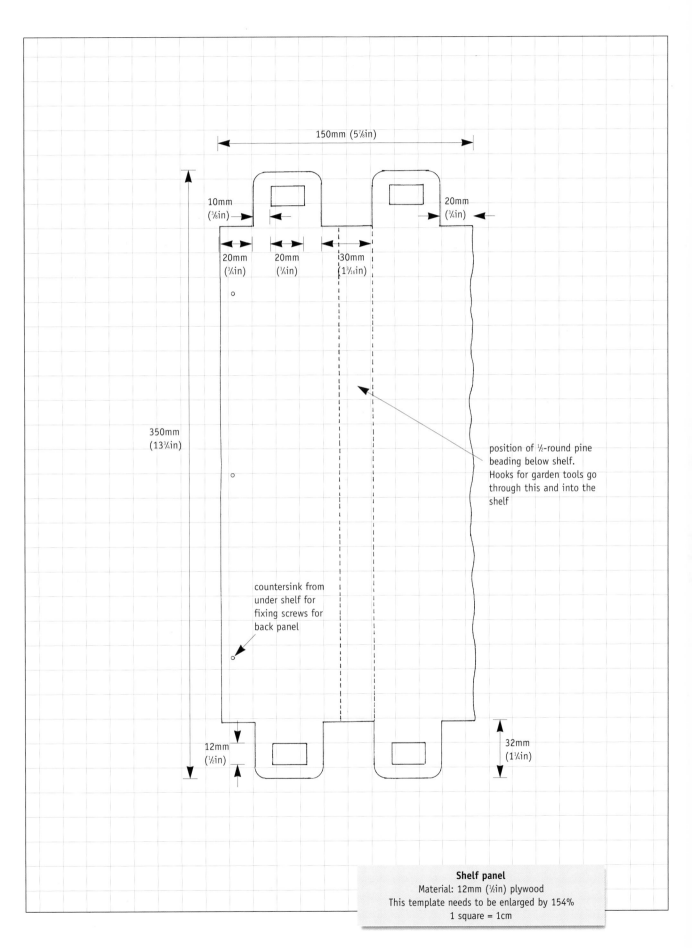

150mm (5⅞in)

10mm (⅜in)

20mm (¾in)

20mm (¾in)

20mm (¾in)

30mm (1³⁄₁₆in)

350mm (13¾in)

position of ½-round pine beading below shelf. Hooks for garden tools go through this and into the shelf

countersink from under shelf for fixing screws for back panel

12mm (½in)

32mm (1¼in)

Shelf panel
Material: 12mm (½in) plywood
This template needs to be enlarged by 154%
1 square = 1cm

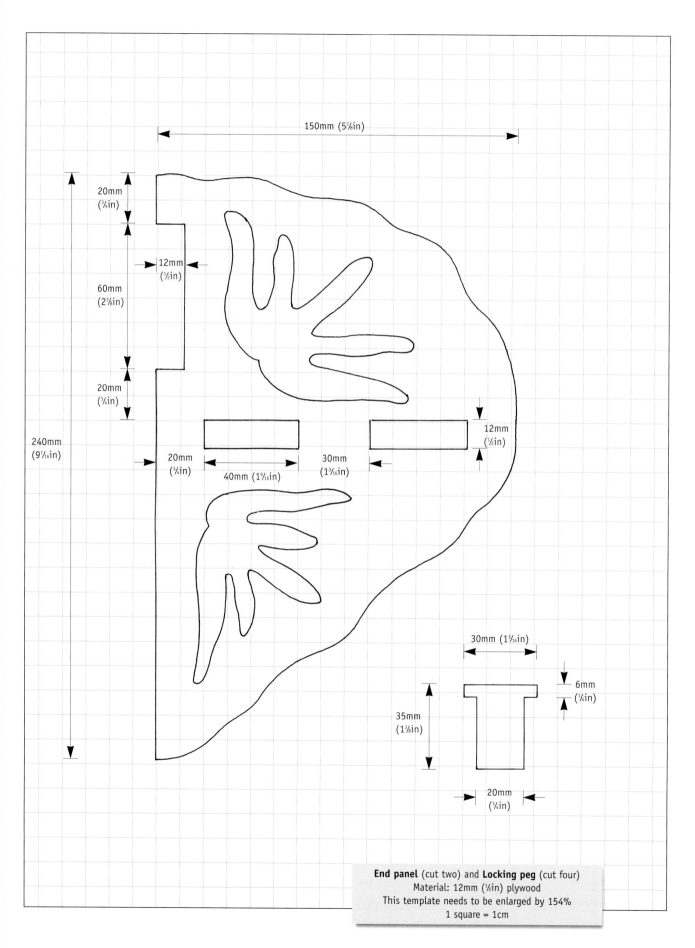

150mm (5⅞in)

20mm
(¾in)

12mm
(½in)

60mm
(2⅜in)

20mm
(¾in)

240mm
(9⁷⁄₁₆in)

20mm
(¾in)

40mm (1⁹⁄₁₆in)

30mm
(1³⁄₁₆in)

12mm
(½in)

30mm (1³⁄₁₆in)

6mm
(¼in)

35mm
(1⅜in)

20mm
(¾in)

End panel (cut two) and **Locking peg** (cut four)
Material: 12mm (½in) plywood
This template needs to be enlarged by 154%
1 square = 1cm

Knick-knack box

This box has two sizes of internal compartments, to accommodate interesting items of varying sizes.

The actual 'body' of the box is laminated from three separate pieces of wood. This is stronger than using a single piece of timber of equivalent thickness, and helps to eliminate warping or twisting of the completed box. No woodworking joints are needed, as the internal compartments are cut out from the 'solid'.

The lid is decorated with a small intarsia design of a rose, and is fixed to the body of the box with small brass hinges. The base has a sheet of thin cork (available from DIY outlets and most hobby stores) bonded to the underside, to prevent scratching of polished surfaces.

The completed knick-knack box showing the intarsia rose in its place

The internal layout of the box

The body of the box cut out, showing the sandwich of wood and the parts for the intarsia 'rose and leaves' which will adorn the top of the completed box

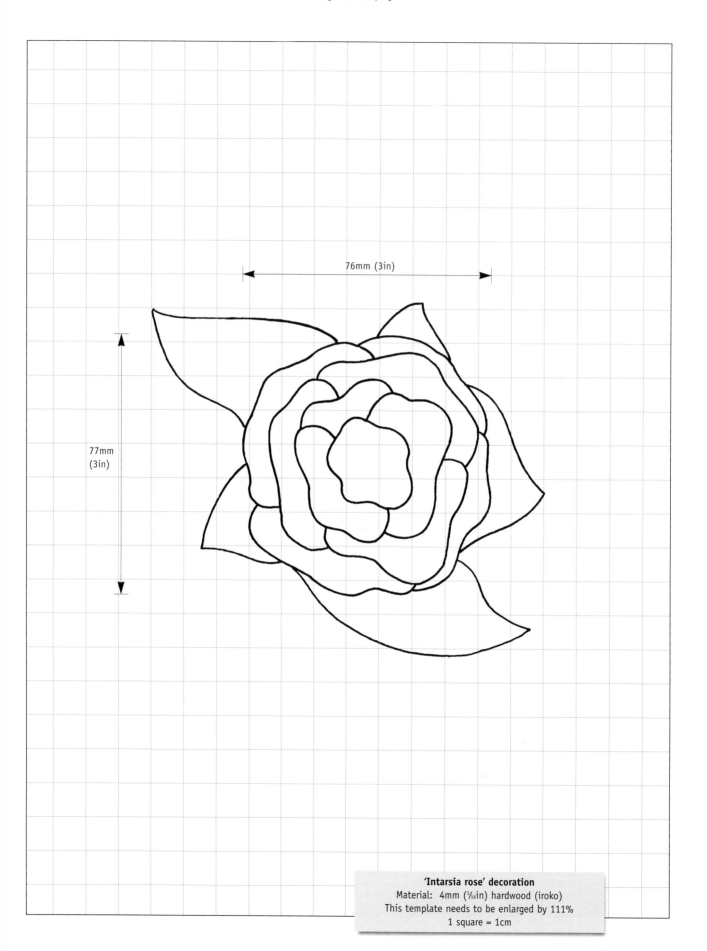

76mm (3in)

77mm
(3in)

'Intarsia rose' decoration
Material: 4mm (³⁄₁₆in) hardwood (iroko)
This template needs to be enlarged by 111%
1 square = 1cm

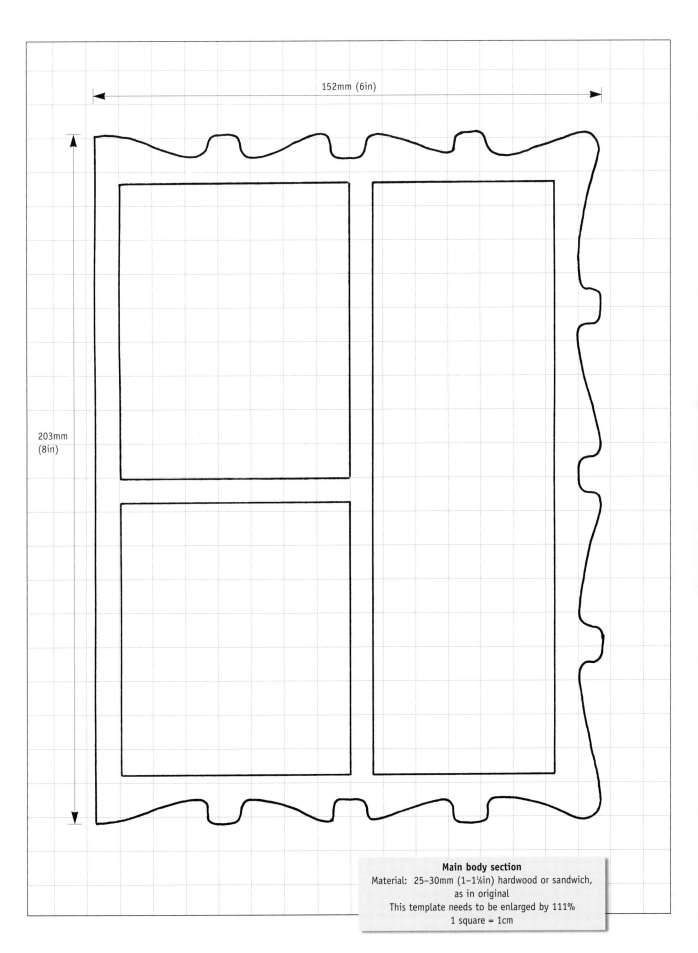

152mm (6in)

203mm
(8in)

Main body section
Material: 25–30mm (1–1⅛in) hardwood or sandwich,
as in original
This template needs to be enlarged by 111%
1 square = 1cm

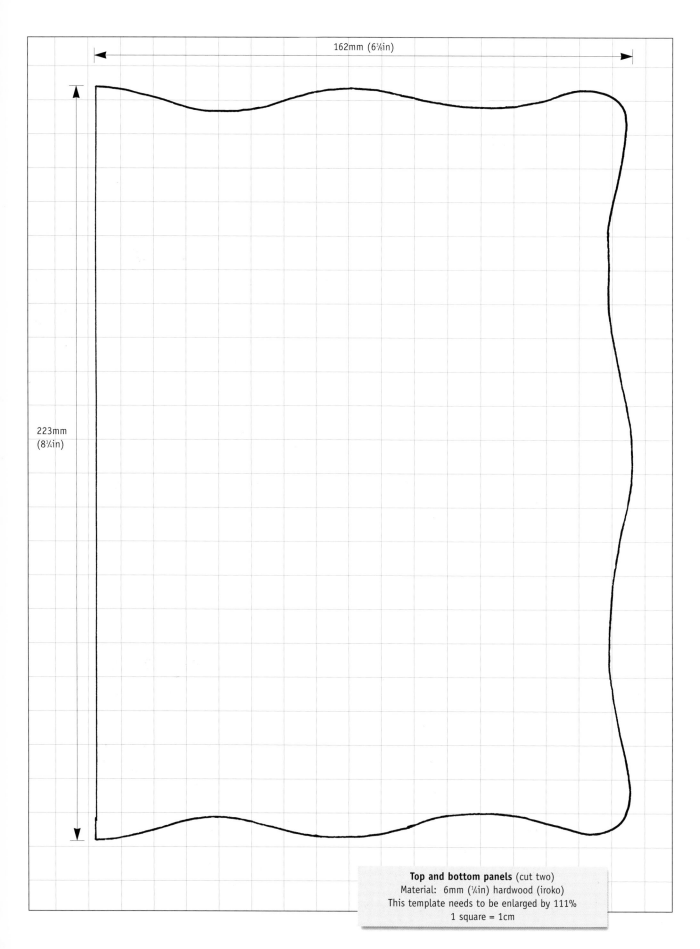

162mm (6⅜in)

223mm
(8¾in)

Top and bottom panels (cut two)
Material: 6mm (¼in) hardwood (iroko)
This template needs to be enlarged by 111%
1 square = 1cm

Potpourri casket

This little casket makes an attractive container for potpourri. The lid is decorated with an intarsia flower, and the casket has cutouts in the side panels and the lid, to allow the scent to pervade the room. The project is straightforward to cut out, although a degree of accuracy is needed.

For best results, assemble the components in the following sequence:

   i) glue the octagonal side panel support to the base panel

   ii) assemble the intarsia decoration for the lid and glue it in place on the lower lid panel

   iii) glue the side panels in place around the octagonal support, using a strong elastic band to hold them in place while the adhesive sets

The completed potpourri casket with its contents

   iv) add the upper support for the side panels, remembering to set it low enough to allow the lid to fit properly.

Apply polish, varnish or teak oil and your casket is complete.

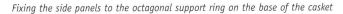

Fixing the side panels to the octagonal support ring on the base of the casket

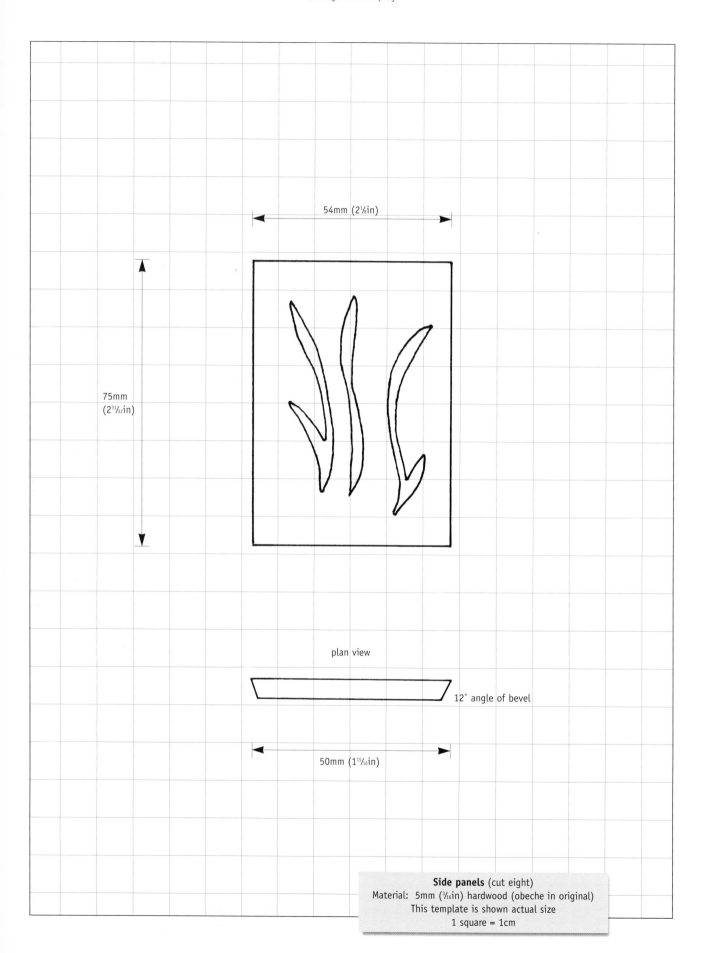

54mm (2⅛in)

75mm
(2³¹⁄₃₂in)

plan view

12° angle of bevel

50mm (1¹⁵⁄₁₆in)

Side panels (cut eight)
Material: 5mm (³⁄₁₆in) hardwood (obeche in original)
This template is shown actual size
1 square = 1cm

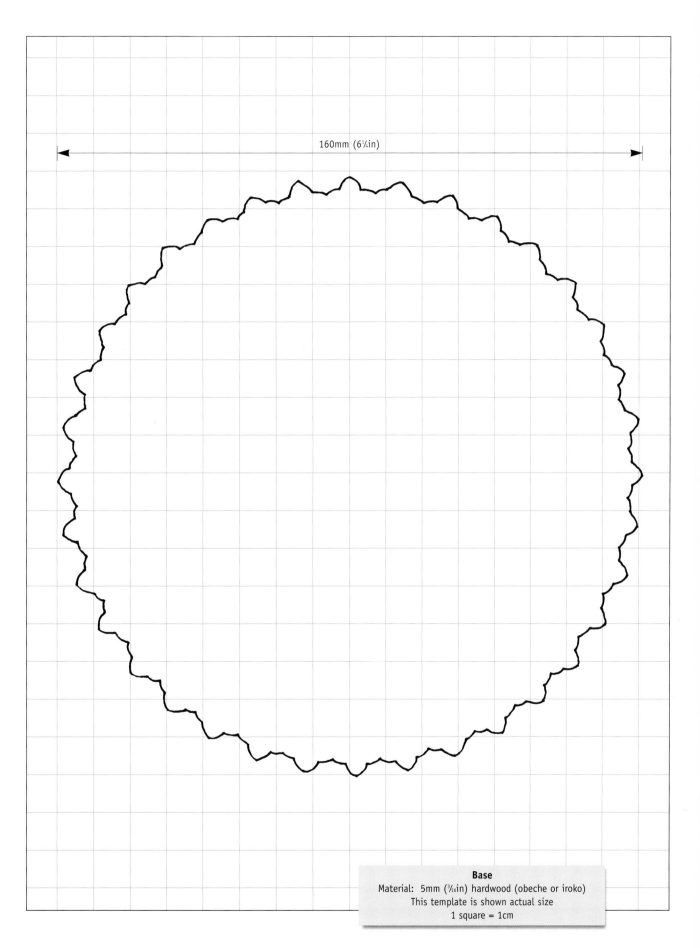

160mm (6¼in)

Base
Material: 5mm (³⁄₁₆in) hardwood (obeche or iroko)
This template is shown actual size
1 square = 1cm

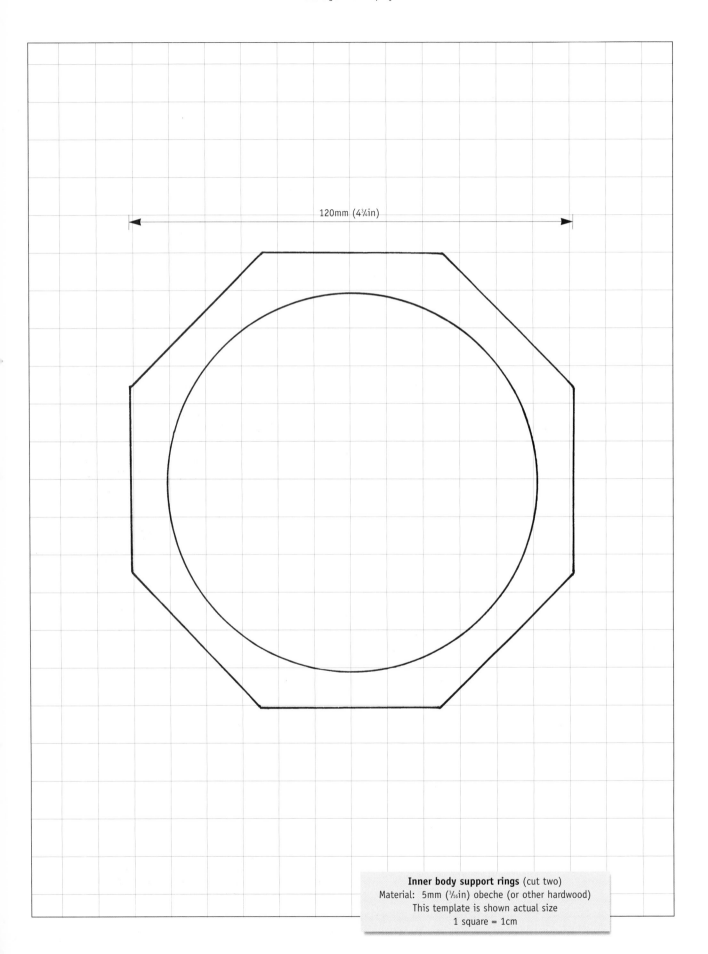

120mm (4¾in)

Inner body support rings (cut two)
Material: 5mm (³⁄₁₆in) obeche (or other hardwood)
This template is shown actual size
1 square = 1cm

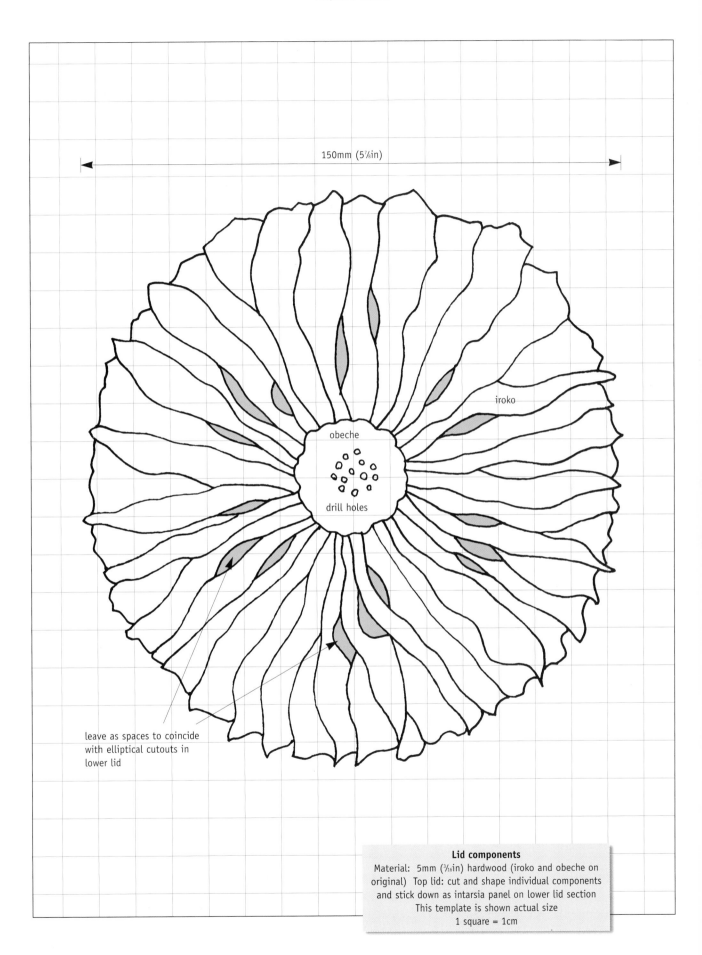

150mm (5⅞in)

iroko

obeche

drill holes

leave as spaces to coincide
with elliptical cutouts in
lower lid

Lid components
Material: 5mm (³⁄₁₆in) hardwood (iroko and obeche on
original) Top lid: cut and shape individual components
and stick down as intarsia panel on lower lid section
This template is shown actual size
1 square = 1cm

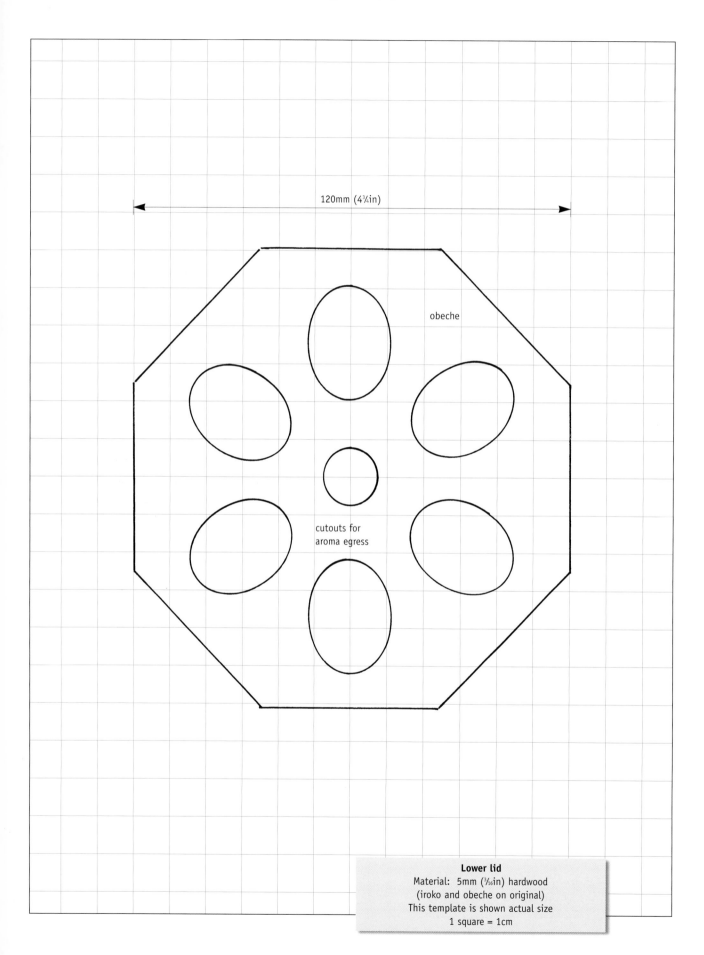

120mm (4¾in)

obeche

cutouts for
aroma egress

Lower lid
Material: 5mm (³⁄₁₆in) hardwood
(iroko and obeche on original)
This template is shown actual size
1 square = 1cm

Pair of candle holders

The wooden parts of these candle holders are straightforward to cut out and you can, if you like, make all the parts from wood. However, the tops of those illustrated were made from scrap pieces of roofing slate, which add an interesting contrast. Not only does the slate look good, it will also retain any falling wax from the candles and it is, of course, non-flammable.

To prepare the broken slate, first smooth the surfaces off a little with emery paper. Next, place the slate on a scrap of thin ply or similar. This will prevent any breakout from the underside as you cut around the pattern and will also protect the surface of your saw's work table, which might otherwise become scratched if any roughness is left on the slate.

Use a tungsten carbide tile saw blade – obtainable from any DIY store – to cut the slate. If your saw will not accept this length of pin-end blade, you can snap the blade off to length, and grind a flat that will fit into the blade holders of your own saw.

The completed candle holders with candles in place

Cutting the circle for the candle from a piece of scrap slate. Note the use of scrap ply which prevents the slate flaking as it is cut, and protects the saw work table

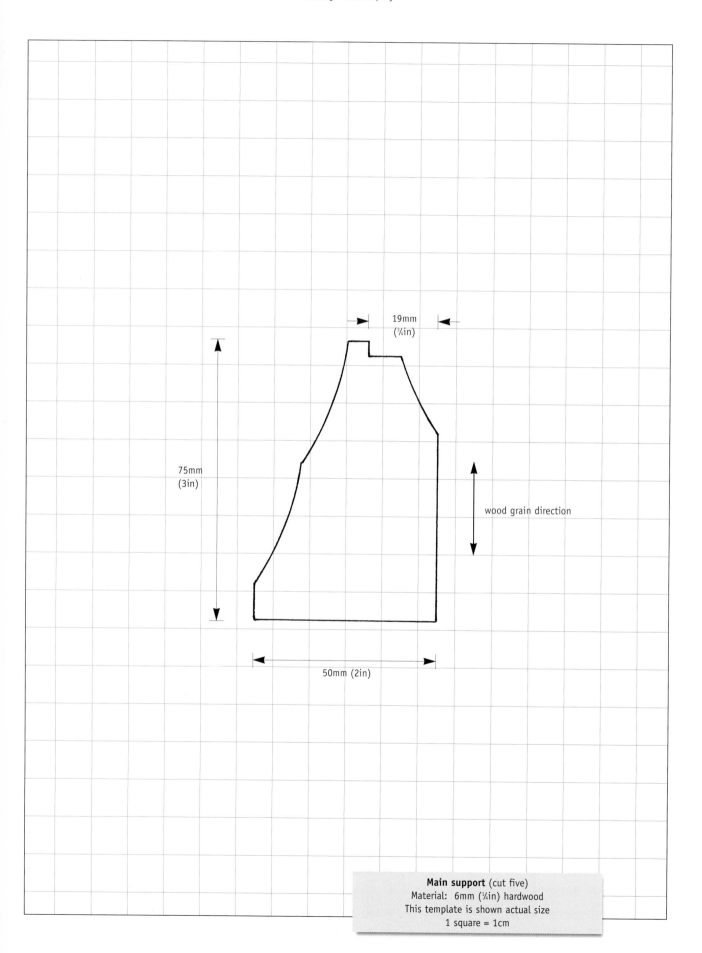

19mm
(¾in)

75mm
(3in)

wood grain direction

50mm (2in)

Main support (cut five)
Material: 6mm (¼in) hardwood
This template is shown actual size
1 square = 1cm

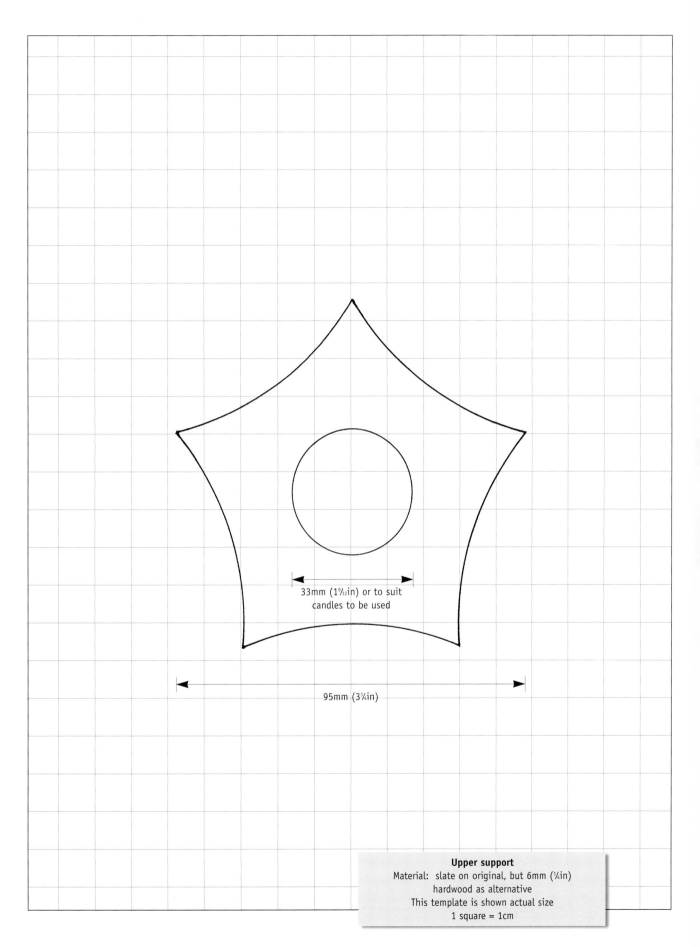

33mm (1⁹⁄₃₂in) or to suit
candles to be used

95mm (3¾in)

Upper support
Material: slate on original, but 6mm (¼in)
hardwood as alternative
This template is shown actual size
1 square = 1cm

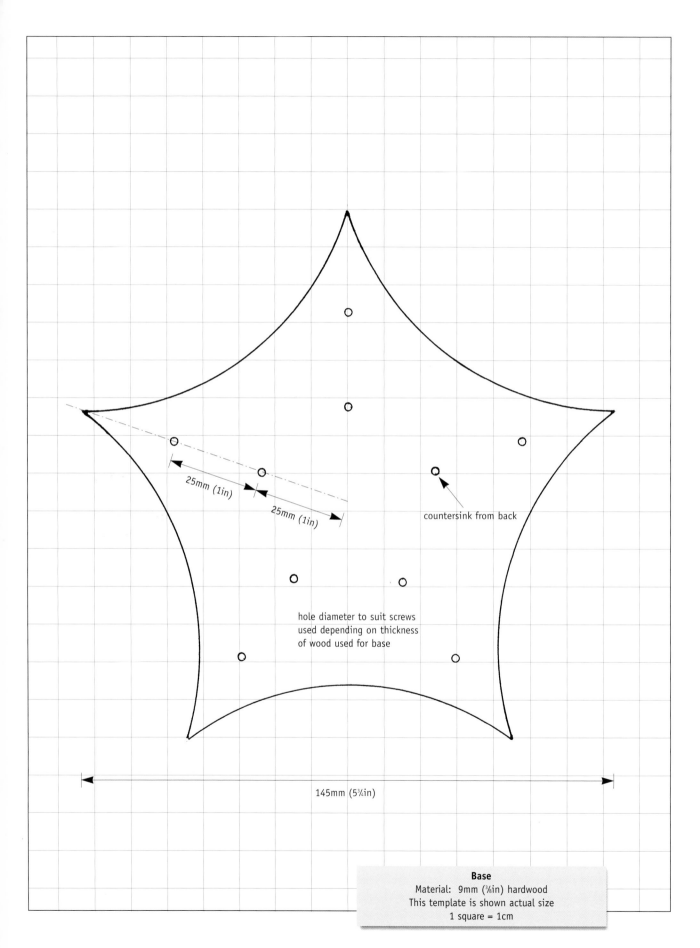

25mm (1in)

25mm (1in)

countersink from back

hole diameter to suit screws
used depending on thickness
of wood used for base

145mm (5¾in)

Base
Material: 9mm (⅜in) hardwood
This template is shown actual size
1 square = 1cm

Floating candle bowl stand

The completed project with its floating candle

This project makes an attractive centrepiece for a table.

Carefully check the dimensions and interior shape of the components of the stand against the bowl you intend to use, as the dimensions of your bowl may differ widely from the one used here. Do this before actually gluing the two halves of the stand together, so that any adjustments to the curvature of the inner surface of the rack can be made more easily. However, the basic design – which lifts the bowl clear of the table and protects the table surface from water spillages – will, of course, remain the same.

The original shown here was made from two small pieces of oak recovered from an old drawer. The blank material was carefully sanded smooth, cut out and then varnished to protect it from water spills.

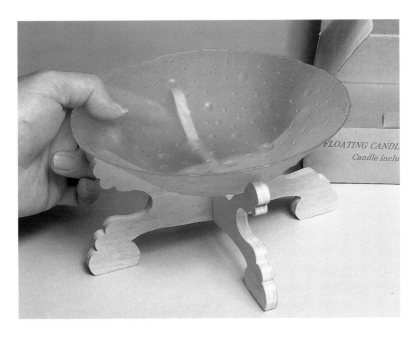

Checking the bowl for an accurate fit on its stand

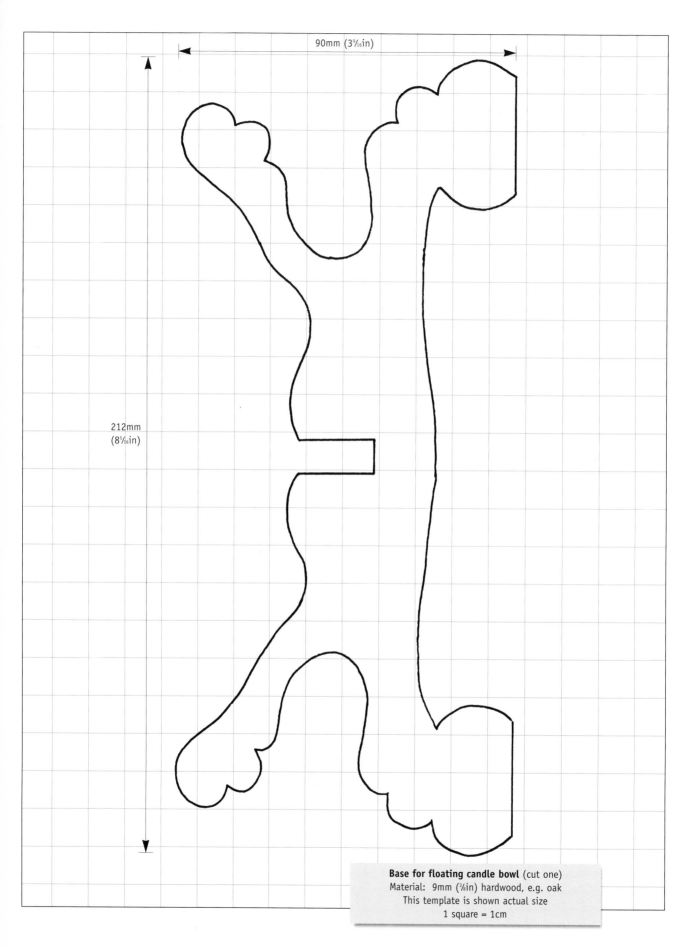

90mm (3⁹⁄₁₆in)

212mm
(8⁵⁄₁₆in)

Base for floating candle bowl (cut one)
Material: 9mm (³⁄₈in) hardwood, e.g. oak
This template is shown actual size
1 square = 1cm

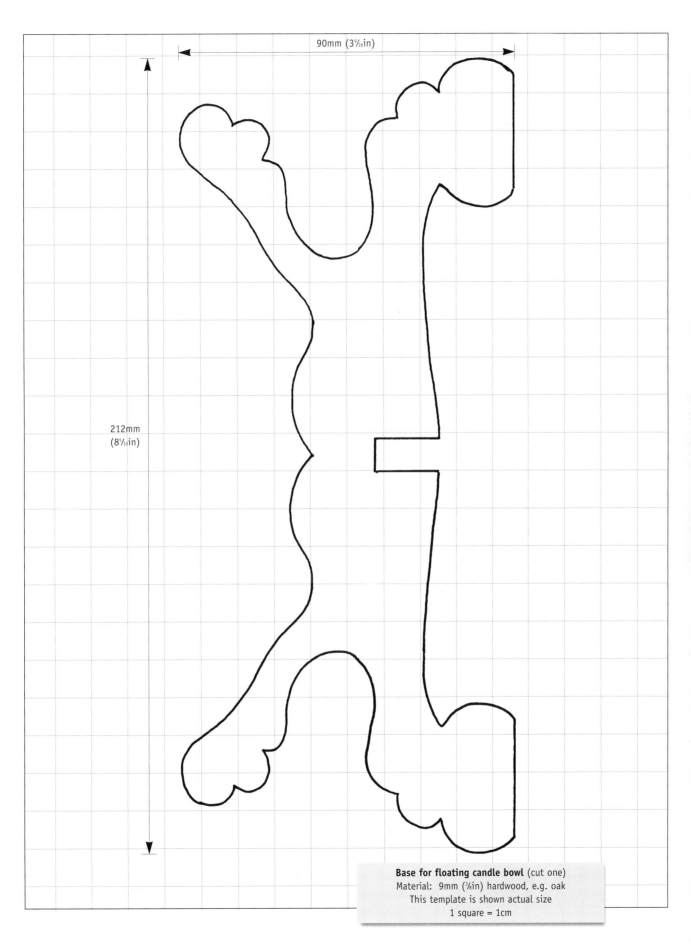

90mm (3⁹⁄₁₆in)

212mm
(8⁵⁄₁₆in)

Base for floating candle bowl (cut one)
Material: 9mm (³⁄₈in) hardwood, e.g. oak
This template is shown actual size
1 square = 1cm

Ornament scales

The completed scales. As a finishing touch, I have added a set of brass feet, originally intended for a clock case

These scales are perfect for displaying ornaments, such as the pyramids of cut glass and stone shown here. These pyramids are quite heavy for their size, so the scales must be able to support a reasonable weight. The balance arm is fixed, so there is no danger of tipping valuable ornaments over when in use, and the scale pans are attached to the balance arm with thin chain and ring pins, which are obtainable from craft shops and craft jewellery suppliers.

A few miniature tools – such as wire cutters and jewellers' pliers – are useful, as the chains must be identical lengths for the scale pans to hang correctly, and the shanks of the ring pins may well need to be cut down before use. Approximately 12mm (½in) of shank is needed on each ring pin to ensure adequate support for the scale pan when loaded with an ornament.

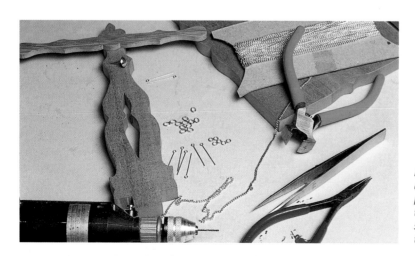

Making up the scale pans, prior to assembling to the balance arm. The ring pins and chains are shown, together with the miniature tools used for the assembly stage. Complete assembly before inserting the scale unit into its base

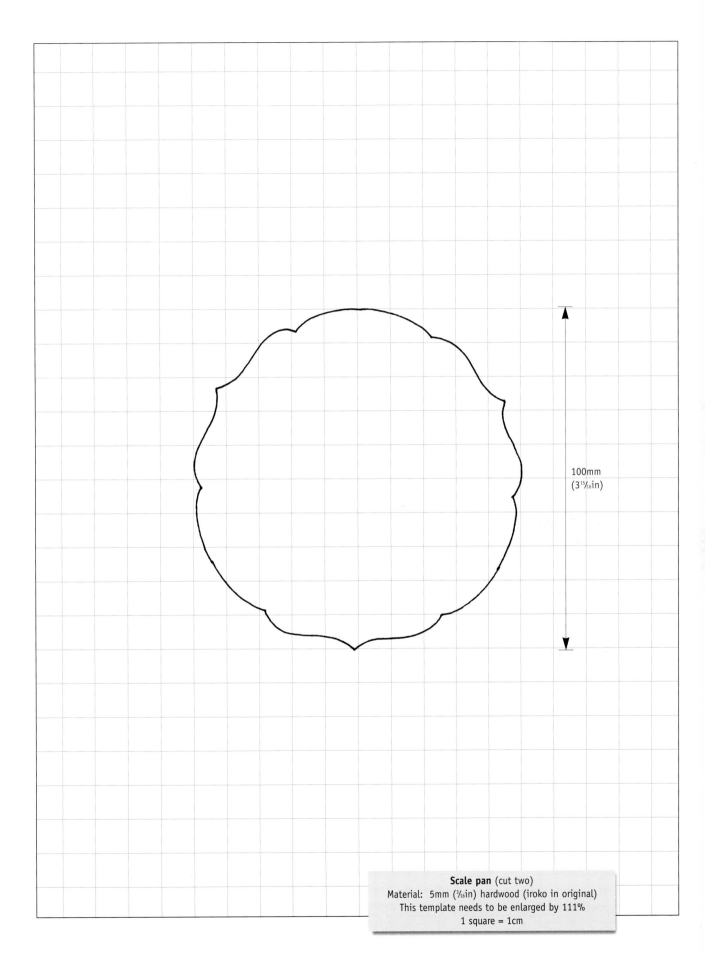

100mm
(3¹⁵⁄₁₆in)

Scale pan (cut two)
Material: 5mm (³⁄₁₆in) hardwood (iroko in original)
This template needs to be enlarged by 111%
1 square = 1cm

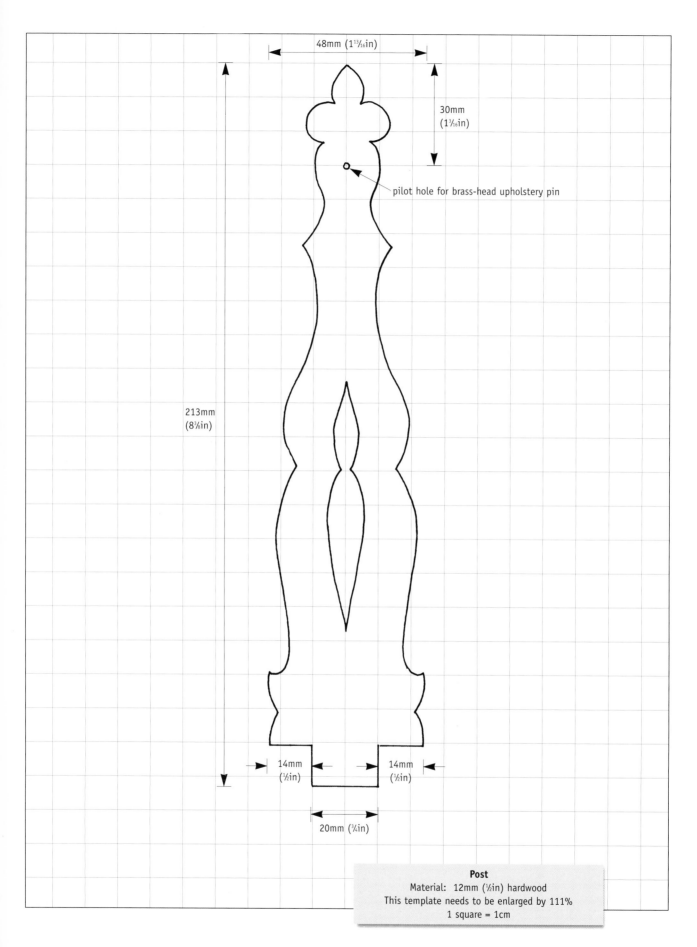

48mm (1¹³⁄₁₆in)

30mm
(1³⁄₁₆in)

pilot hole for brass-head upholstery pin

213mm
(8⅜in)

14mm
(½in)

14mm
(½in)

20mm (¾in)

Post
Material: 12mm (½in) hardwood
This template needs to be enlarged by 111%
1 square = 1cm

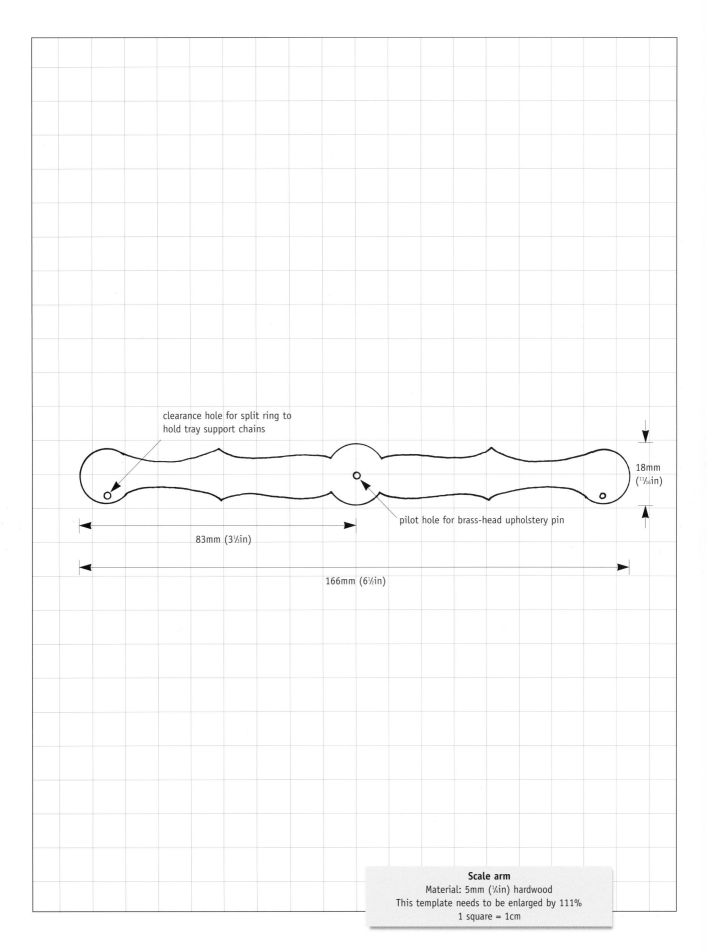

clearance hole for split ring to
hold tray support chains

pilot hole for brass-head upholstery pin

18mm
($^{11}/_{16}$in)

83mm (3$^1/_3$in)

166mm (6$^1/_2$in)

Scale arm
Material: 5mm ($^1/_4$in) hardwood
This template needs to be enlarged by 111%
1 square = 1cm

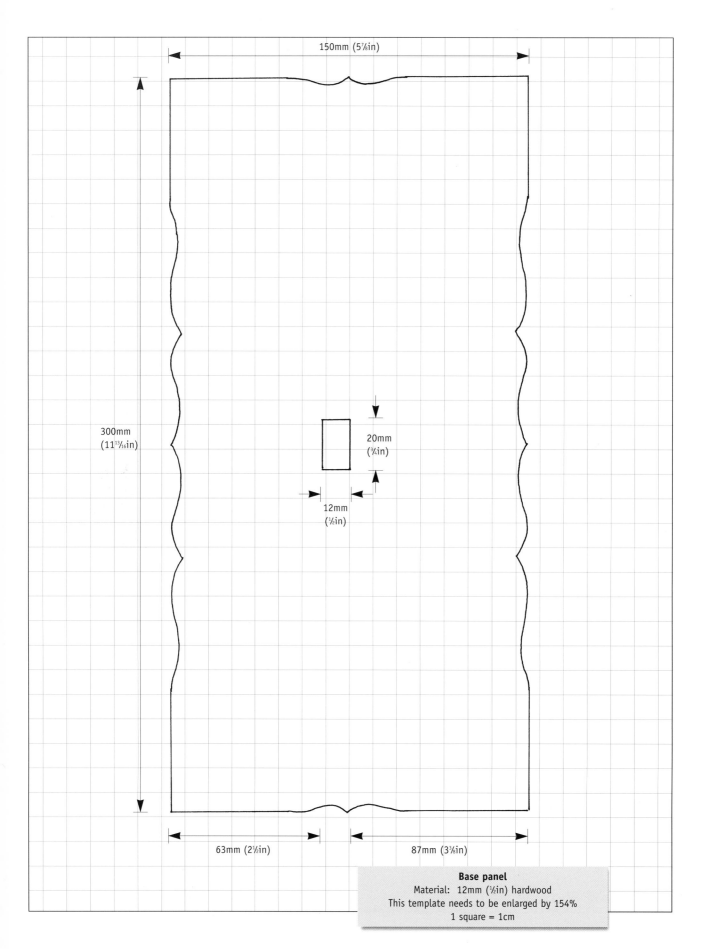

150mm (5⅞in)

300mm
(11¹³⁄₁₆in)

20mm
(¾in)

12mm
(½in)

63mm (2½in)

87mm (3⅜in)

Base panel
Material: 12mm (½in) hardwood
This template needs to be enlarged by 154%
1 square = 1cm

House number plaque

This decorative number plaque was devised as an alternative to the awful plastic versions available in DIY outlets. Contrasting woods were used for the base plate and the overlay piece but paint could be used, to achieve the same effect.

First, stick the cutting pattern for the overlay decoration (but not the numerals) down on the top sheet and make the internal cutouts. Next, place the sheet you have just cut on the blank for the bottom sheet, and cut out the external shape so that the top and bottom pieces will match exactly. Finally, cut out whichever numerals you need, and stick them onto the completed plaque.

Either glue the plaque in place on a wooden door, or secure it with a couple of small brass screws.

The completed door number in place

The internal cutouts on the top sheet have been made, and the stack is ready for cutting out the external shape

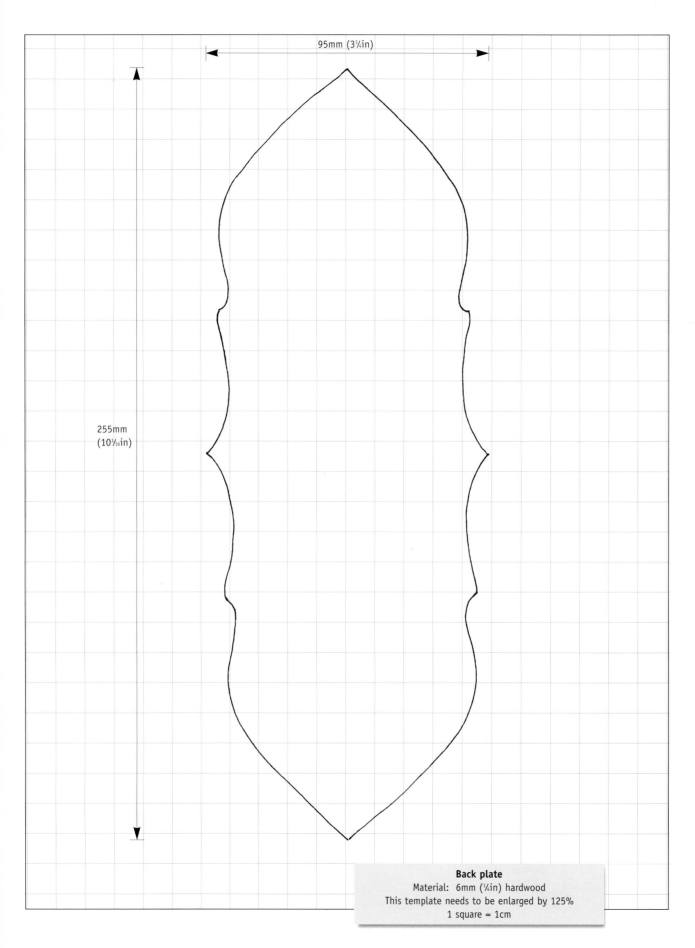

95mm (3¾in)

255mm
(10¹⁄₁₆in)

Back plate
Material: 6mm (¼in) hardwood
This template needs to be enlarged by 125%
1 square = 1cm

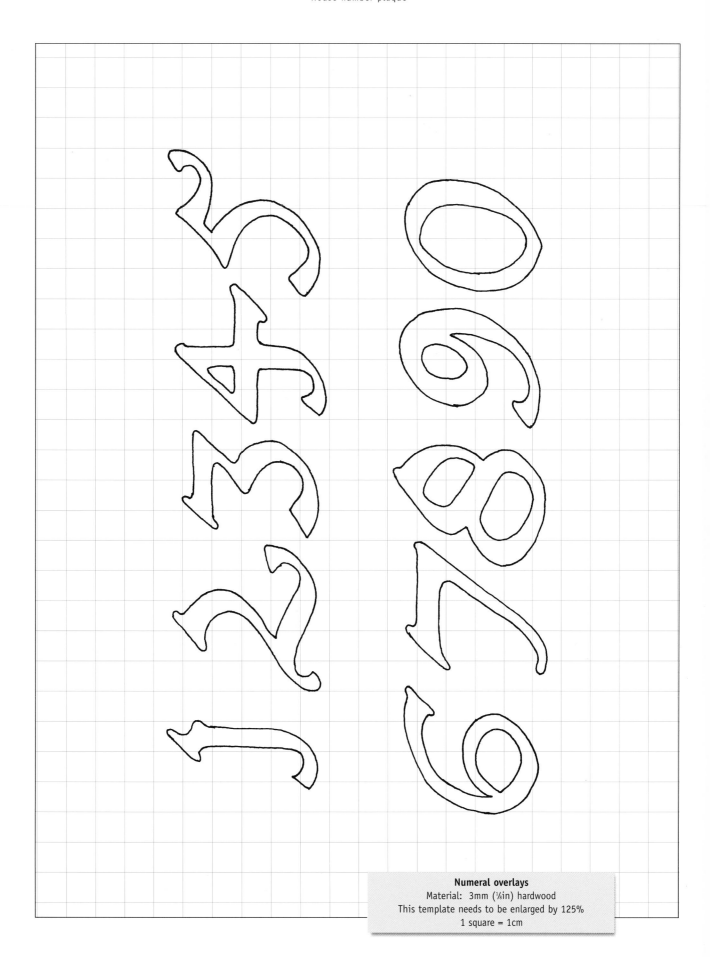

Numeral overlays
Material: 3mm (⅛in) hardwood
This template needs to be enlarged by 125%
1 square = 1cm

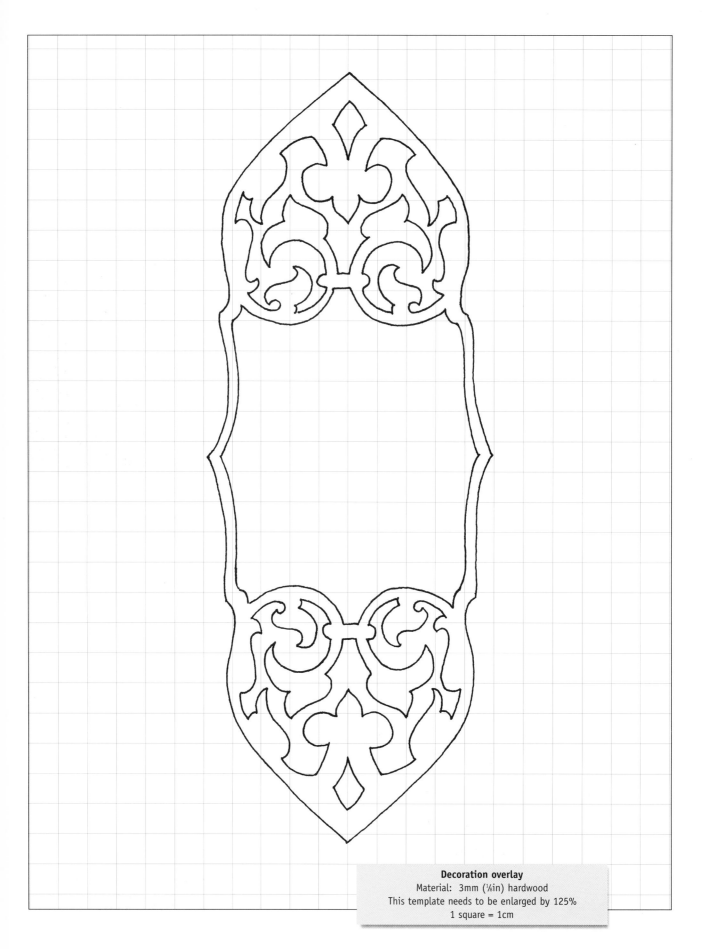

Decoration overlay
Material: 3mm (⅛in) hardwood
This template needs to be enlarged by 125%
1 square = 1cm

Mirror frame

The mirror illustrated was bought cheaply, and its pine frame removed and discarded. It was then given an appealing overlay which is unashamedly 'cottagey' in style.

The main panel is cut to suit the size of mirror to be used. The overlay, consisting of alternate coloured foliage and branches, is cut from thinner material, decorated separately, and then stuck down in position. Make sure that the thickness of wood used for the mirror-retaining frame at the back is of a suitable depth to accommodate the thickness of your chosen mirror – 3mm (⅛in) material will accommodate most inexpensive mirrors.

Do not glue the actual mirror in place, as it could crack with temperature changes. The back panel provides all the support that is necessary. If the mirror is a little loose when the back panel is placed in position, pack out the difference with a thin sheet of card, to hold the mirror firmly but not rigidly.

The completed mirror in position

The main overlay panel has already been painted and the decoupage parts, painted separately, are being added

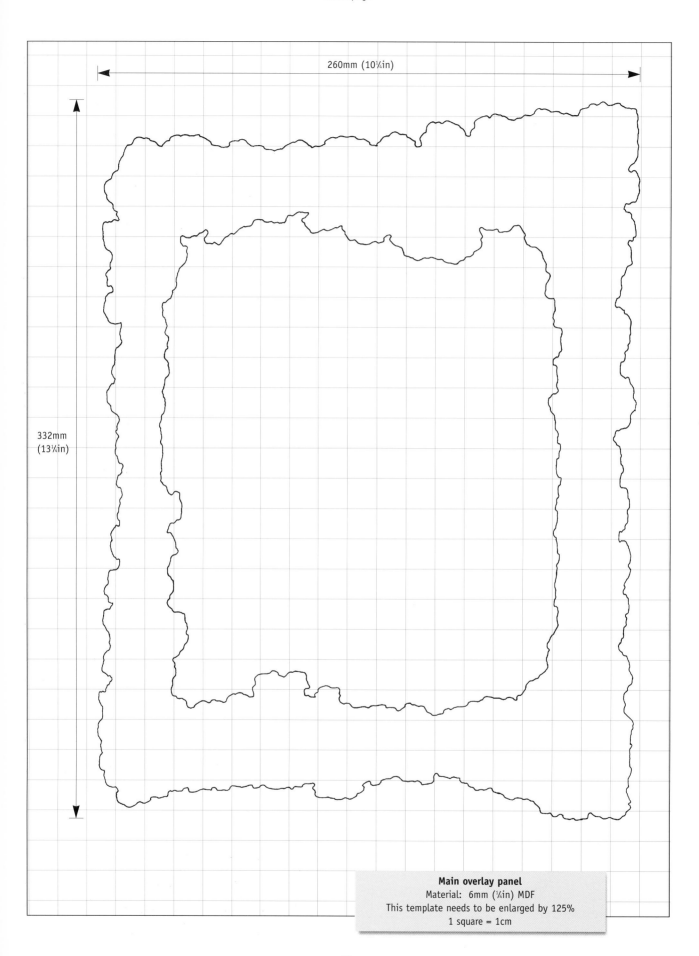

260mm (10¼in)

332mm
(13¼in)

Main overlay panel
Material: 6mm (¼in) MDF
This template needs to be enlarged by 125%
1 square = 1cm

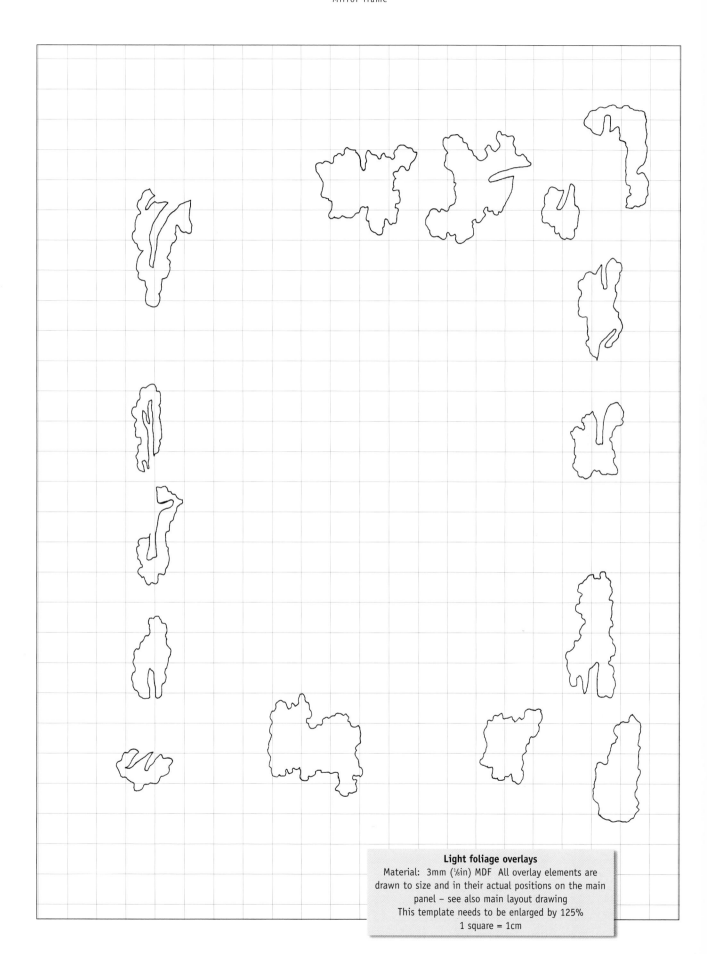

Light foliage overlays
Material: 3mm (⅛in) MDF All overlay elements are
drawn to size and in their actual positions on the main
panel – see also main layout drawing
This template needs to be enlarged by 125%
1 square = 1cm

Branches overlay
Material: 3mm (⅛in) MDF All overlay elements are drawn to size and in their actual positions on the main panel – see also main layout drawing
This template needs to be enlarged by 125%
1 square = 1cm

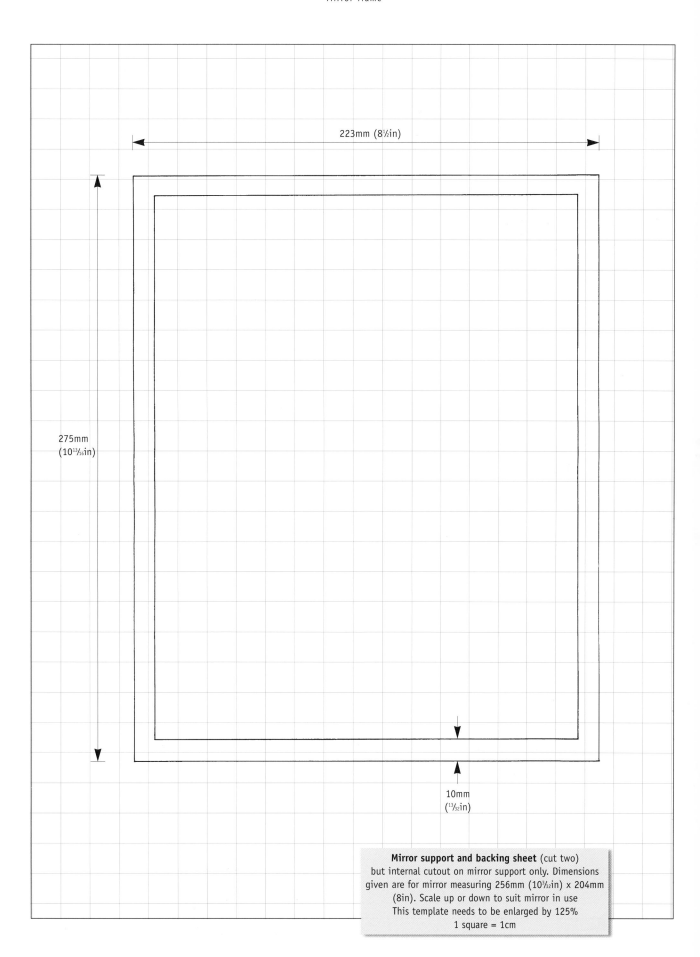

223mm (8½in)

275mm
(10¹³⁄₁₆in)

10mm
(¹³⁄₃₂in)

Mirror support and backing sheet (cut two)
but internal cutout on mirror support only. Dimensions
given are for mirror measuring 256mm (10³⁄₃₂in) x 204mm
(8in). Scale up or down to suit mirror in use
This template needs to be enlarged by 125%
1 square = 1cm

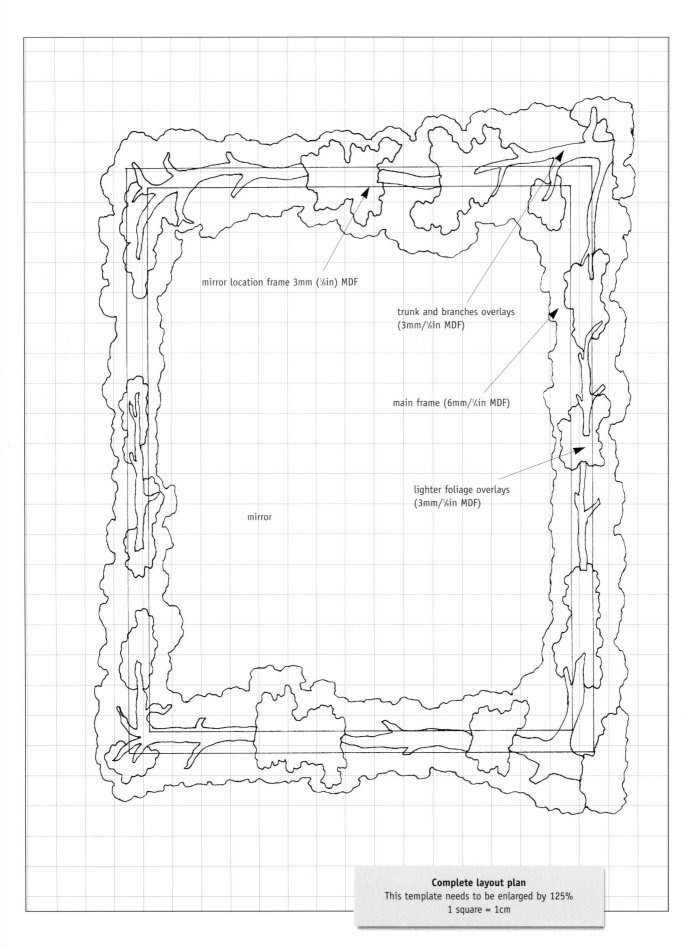

mirror location frame 3mm (⅛in) MDF

trunk and branches overlays
(3mm/⅛in MDF)

main frame (6mm/¼in MDF)

lighter foliage overlays
(3mm/⅛in MDF)

mirror

Complete layout plan
This template needs to be enlarged by 125%
1 square = 1cm

'Gears' picture panel

This interesting project will need accuracy and careful attention to detail to produce a good result, but there are no thicknesses for materials given on the drawings as these are purely arbitrary. The project is useful for turning scraps of hardwood – which are too good to throw away – into a worthwhile product. Use whatever offcuts you have and, if you have several different varieties of hardwood offcut, so much the better to produce variation in the colouring of the final picture.

First make up the frame and backing sheet together, so that you can lay each piece in position as it is cut out, and check for accuracy of fit within the picture.

It is helpful to have an extra copy of the picture layout to hand, so you can check that each piece interlocks correctly with its neighbour as you go along.

The completed gear wheel picture

Matching the offcuts with each item in the cutting pattern, to check for fit prior to cutting out the picture elements

Cutting pattern
Materials: offcuts of wood, metal, plastics, etc
This template needs to be enlarged by 118%
1 square = 1cm

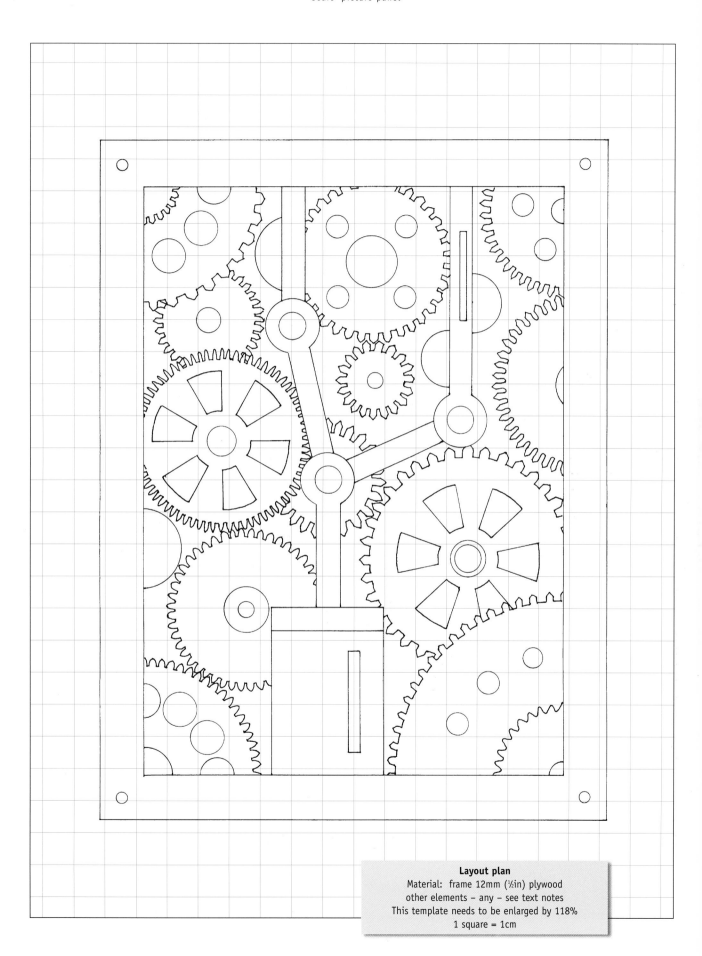

Layout plan
Material: frame 12mm (½in) plywood
other elements – any – see text notes
This template needs to be enlarged by 118%
1 square = 1cm

Note: with all intarsia panels, it is easier working if you have a couple of spare copies of the cutting pattern as layout guides. You can then place the components in their correct places and check that they interlock as you work, which saves having to complete the jigsaw puzzle later on.

Butterflies and daisies

This is the simplest of the intarsia panels in this book but it is, nonetheless, quite challenging, and a little care is needed when cutting out, rounding off and reassembling. Also, beware of small parts within the design getting lost through the blade hole in the saw table.

Most materials can be used to make these intarsia panels, although the examples shown here were made from 6mm (¼in) MDF.

The finished panel

Cutting out the design components and laying them in their correct places on a spare cutting pattern

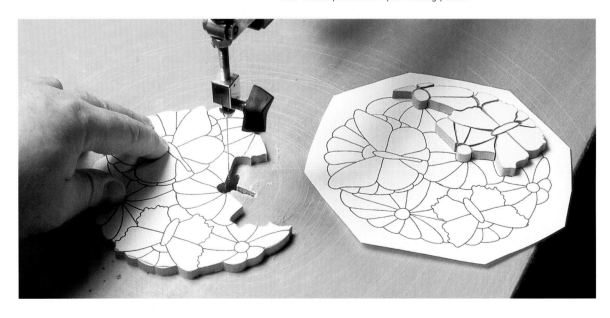

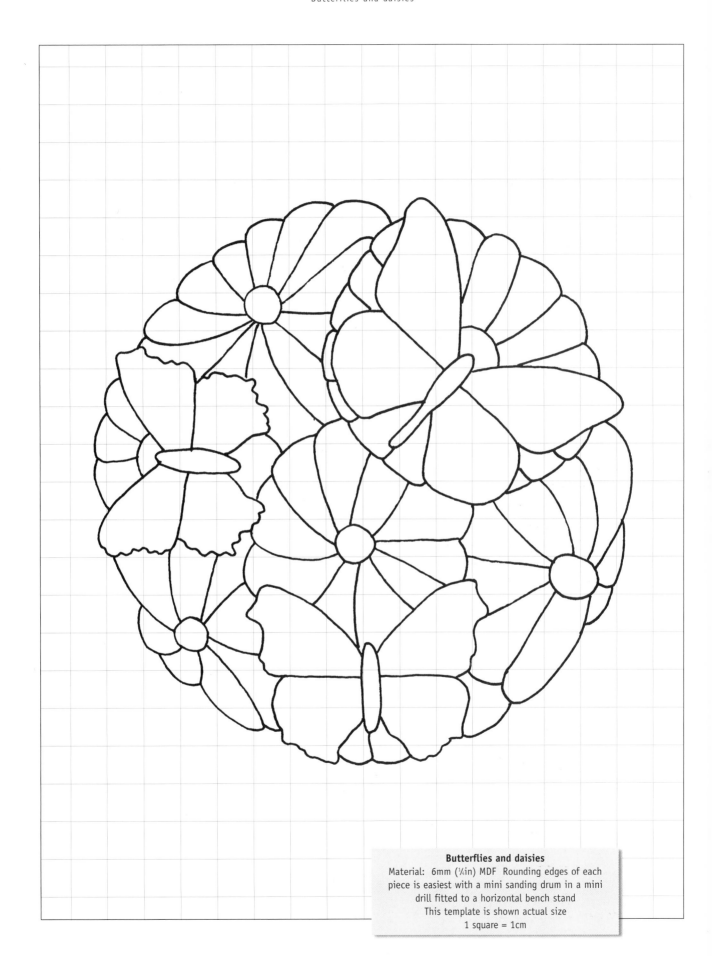

Butterflies and daisies
Material: 6mm (¼in) MDF Rounding edges of each
piece is easiest with a mini sanding drum in a mini
drill fitted to a horizontal bench stand
This template is shown actual size
1 square = 1cm

Geometric panel/place mat

This geometric intarsia panel could well be made up in sets of, say, six completed items for use as place mats, providing a distinctive dining table layout.

Spare copies of the cutting pattern are particularly useful in the case of regular geometric patterns such as this one, as many of the parts are either similar or identical.

The completed item

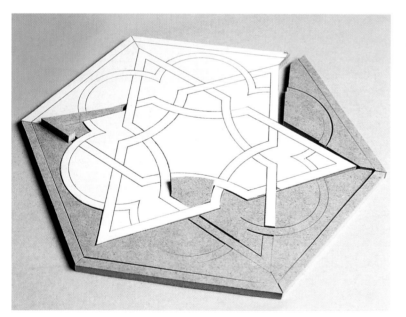

Laying out each part on the spare pattern as it is cut out, so that the fit and correct positioning can be checked within the frame of the design

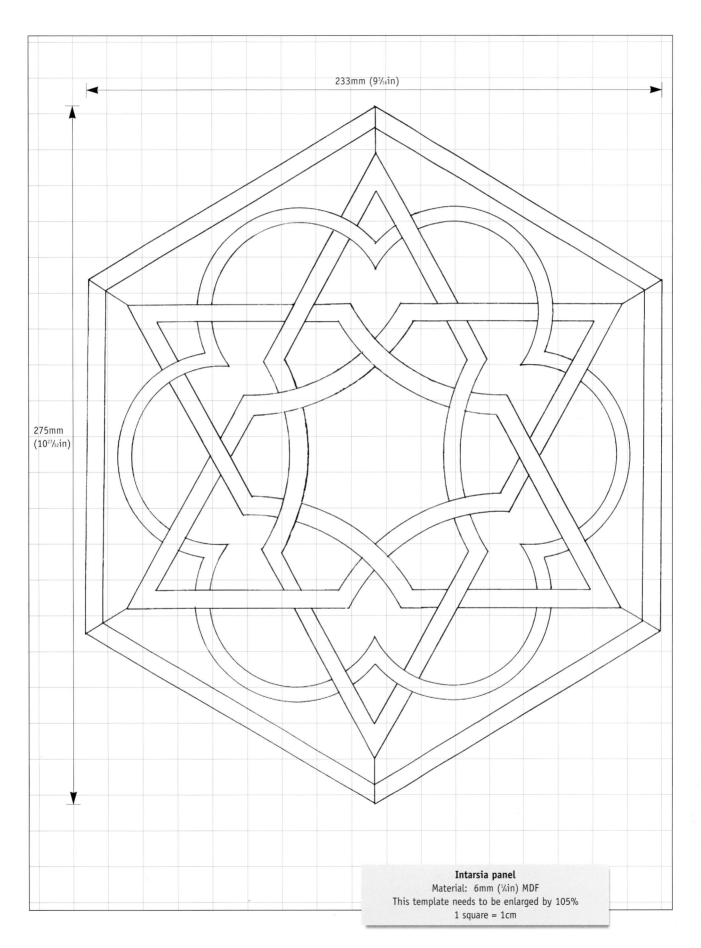

233mm (9³⁄₁₆in)

275mm
(10²⁷⁄₃₂in)

Intarsia panel
Material: 6mm (¼in) MDF
This template needs to be enlarged by 105%
1 square = 1cm

Badgers

The completed badger panel

This panel is the most complex of the three intarsia panels and there are quite a few small parts which will need careful handling at both the sawing and the rounding off stages. To avoid losing small pieces, such as the badgers' noses, use a plastic tray (such as a recycled food container) to catch any wayward bits that fall through the saw blade hole on your work table.

Wooden clothes pegs make effective miniature vices for holding the components while decorating and cost very little to buy.

Using a small round file on components which are too small for even the smallest drum sander

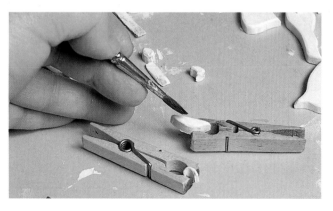

Modified wooden clothes pegs can be used as clamps to hold the smallest pieces for decoration prior to final assembly

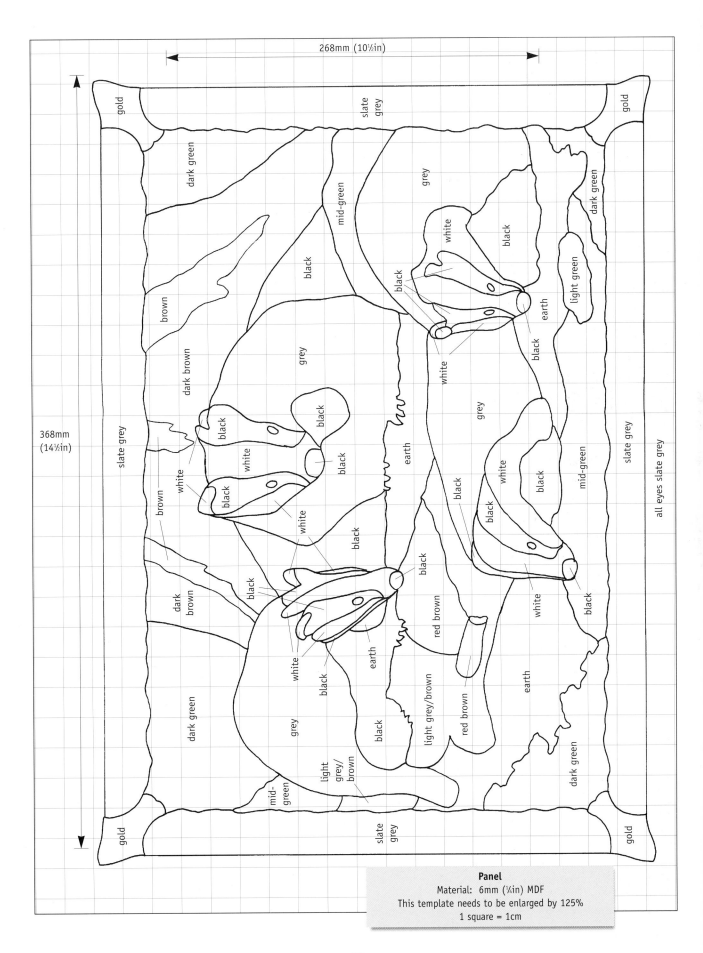

268mm (10½in)

368mm
(14½in)

gold

slate
grey

gold

dark green

slate
grey

grey

dark green

mid-green

white

black

light green

black

brown

black

black

earth

black

grey

dark brown

grey

black

white

grey

black

black

white

white

black

white

black

black

black

earth

slate grey

brown

white

black

white

mid-green

all eyes slate grey

black

white

black

black

black

white

white

black

black

black

black

dark
brown

grey

white

earth

red brown

earth

black

black

dark green

grey

black

light grey/brown

white

dark green

light
grey/
brown

red brown

mid-
green

slate
grey

gold

slate
grey

gold

Panel
Material: 6mm (¼in) MDF
This template needs to be enlarged by 125%
1 square = 1cm

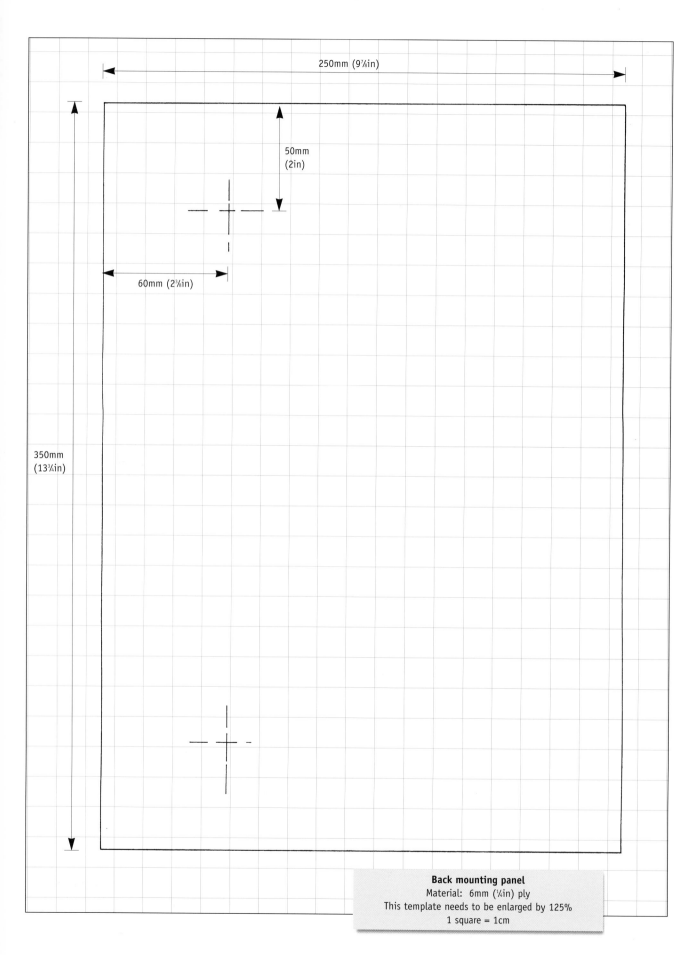

250mm (9⅞in)

50mm
(2in)

60mm (2⅜in)

350mm
(13¾in)

Back mounting panel
Material: 6mm (¼in) ply
This template needs to be enlarged by 125%
1 square = 1cm

Jigsaw puzzle

This project enables you to make a favourite photograph or picture into a fully interlocking jigsaw puzzle. The pattern, which is approximately 254 x 202mm (10 x 8in), produces a puzzle of 108 pieces, which is sufficient to make it interesting for a picture of this size.

First, cut a sheet of 6mm (¼in) MDF to size, then firmly bond your chosen picture to it, using a permanent photomount adhesive. Next, stick the cutting pattern down onto the surface of the picture. Use a very low tack spray adhesive for this, such as ReMount, which will not damage the actual picture when the pattern is removed after cutting out.

A fine blade – around size 2 or less – is ideal for this job, as it won't remove too much material from each cut and the puzzle pieces will remain a good fit.

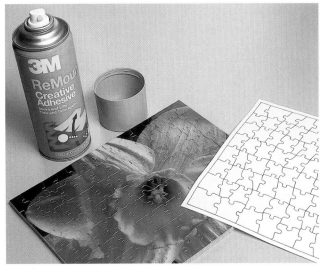

The chosen picture bonded to a sheet of MDF and the cutting pattern ready to be stuck down with low tack Remount adhesive

The completed jigsaw puzzle from a favourite picture

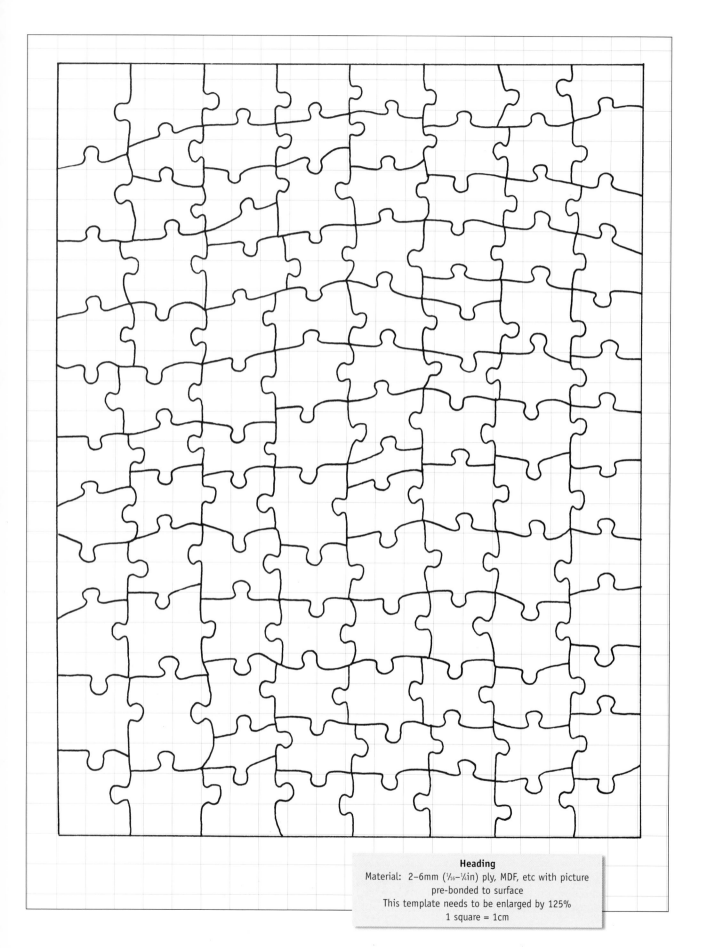

Heading
Material: 2–6mm (¹⁄₁₆–¼in) ply, MDF, etc with picture
pre-bonded to surface
This template needs to be enlarged by 125%
1 square = 1cm

Toy aeroplane

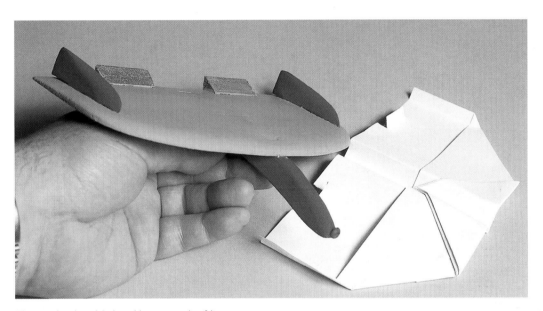

The completed model alongside an example of its paper predecessor

This project was modelled on an old paper aeroplane design which I first made over forty years ago, so it is a fun update of an old concept. It has been developed for making up in balsa wood but retains all the characteristics of the paper version and it flies just as well, too. The thinner parts, especially, will need to be handled with care as balsa has little mechanical strength.

The wing is shaped into an aerofoil section by simply sanding it off to the shape given in the drawings. To enable it to fly properly, a suitable weight must be added to the nose of the aeroplane and it may take a little trial and error to find the right amount of weight for your particular model; the one illustrated had a self-tapping screw added to the very front of the nose, which made for good flying, but a couple of small washers glued into the nose might work just as well.

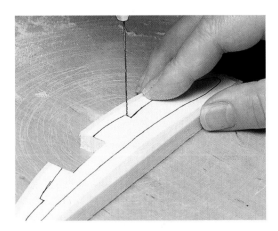

Cutting out the fuselage section from sheet balsa. The joint cutouts must be square into the corners, so that the wing section – which is added later – is a good fit

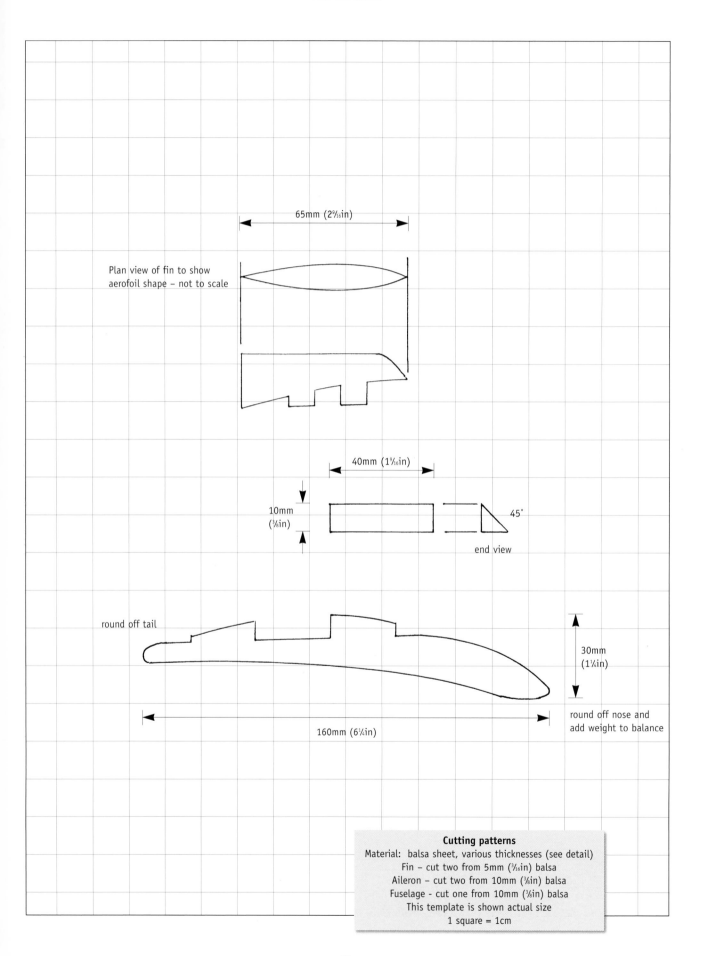

65mm (2⁹⁄₁₆in)

Plan view of fin to show
aerofoil shape – not to scale

40mm (1⁹⁄₁₆in)

10mm
(³⁄₈in)

45°

end view

round off tail

30mm
(1¼in)

160mm (6¼in)

round off nose and
add weight to balance

Cutting patterns
Material: balsa sheet, various thicknesses (see detail)
Fin – cut two from 5mm (³⁄₁₆in) balsa
Aileron – cut two from 10mm (³⁄₈in) balsa
Fuselage - cut one from 10mm (³⁄₈in) balsa
This template is shown actual size
1 square = 1cm

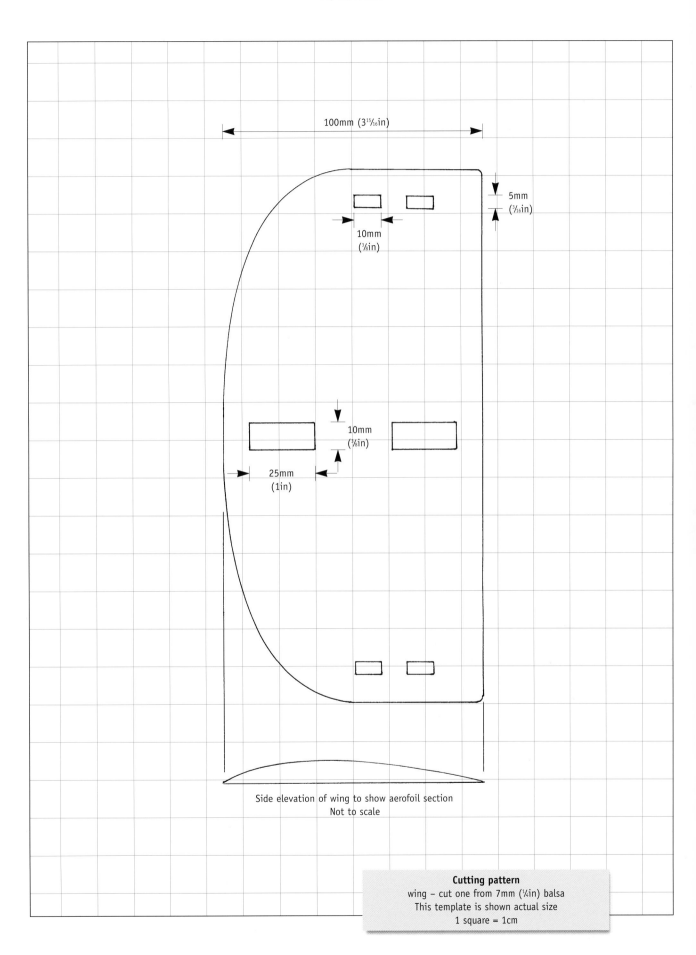

100mm (3¹⁵⁄₁₆in)

5mm
(³⁄₁₆in)

10mm
(³⁄₈in)

10mm
(³⁄₈in)

25mm
(1in)

Side elevation of wing to show aerofoil section
Not to scale

Cutting pattern
wing – cut one from 7mm (¼in) balsa
This template is shown actual size
1 square = 1cm

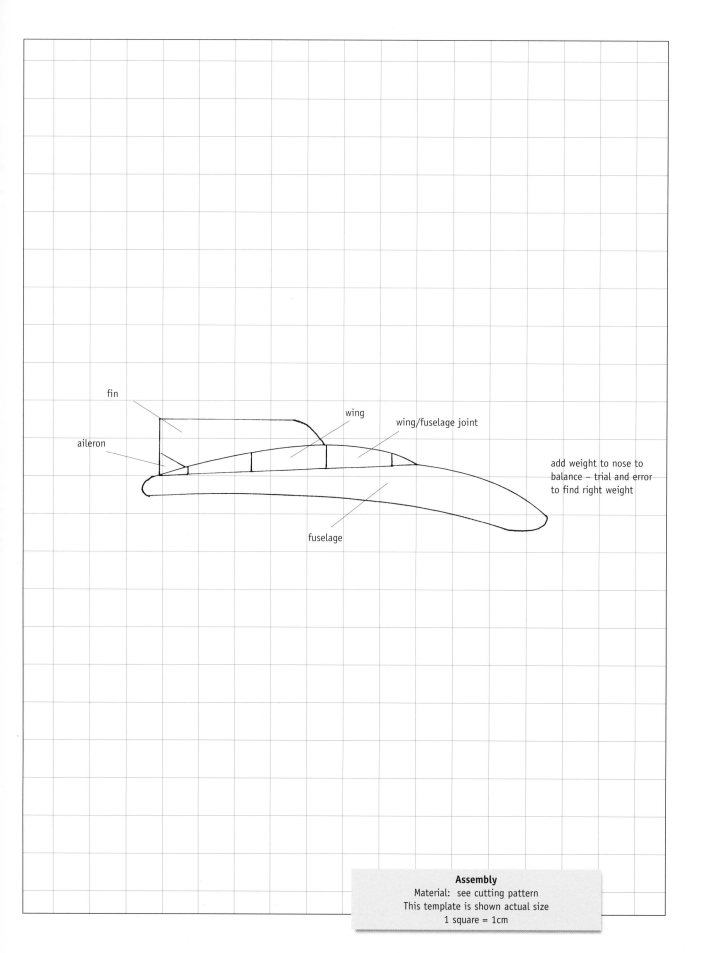

fin

wing

wing/fuselage joint

aileron

add weight to nose to
balance – trial and error
to find right weight

fuselage

Assembly
Material: see cutting pattern
This template is shown actual size
1 square = 1cm

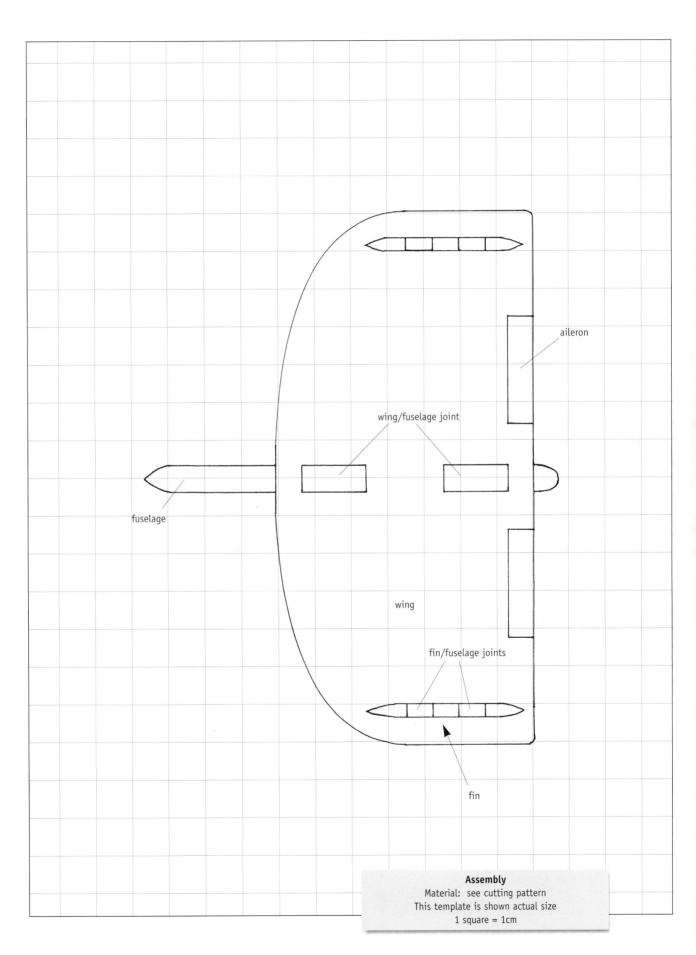

aileron

wing/fuselage joint

fuselage

wing

fin/fuselage joints

fin

Assembly
Material: see cutting pattern
This template is shown actual size
1 square = 1cm

Teleidoscope

This fascinating item is very popular with children (of all ages!) – look at your chosen object through the teleidoscope and you get a kaleidoscopic image of whatever is in view.

The teleidoscope uses the same mirror system as the familiar kaleidoscope, but without the 'cell' on the end which contains the coloured glass chips, etc. The project here uses a small section of plastic 'mirror card' – obtainable from most hobby suppliers – surrounded by a scrollcut framework, which provides both decoration and protection for the mirror system.

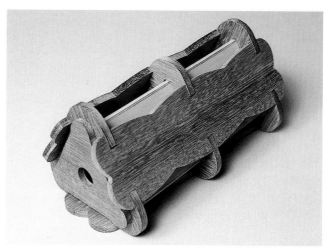

The completed teleidoscope

Checking the framework pieces for accurate fit before finally gluing them in place

Example of a view through the teleidoscope, taken with a camera looking through the 'business end'

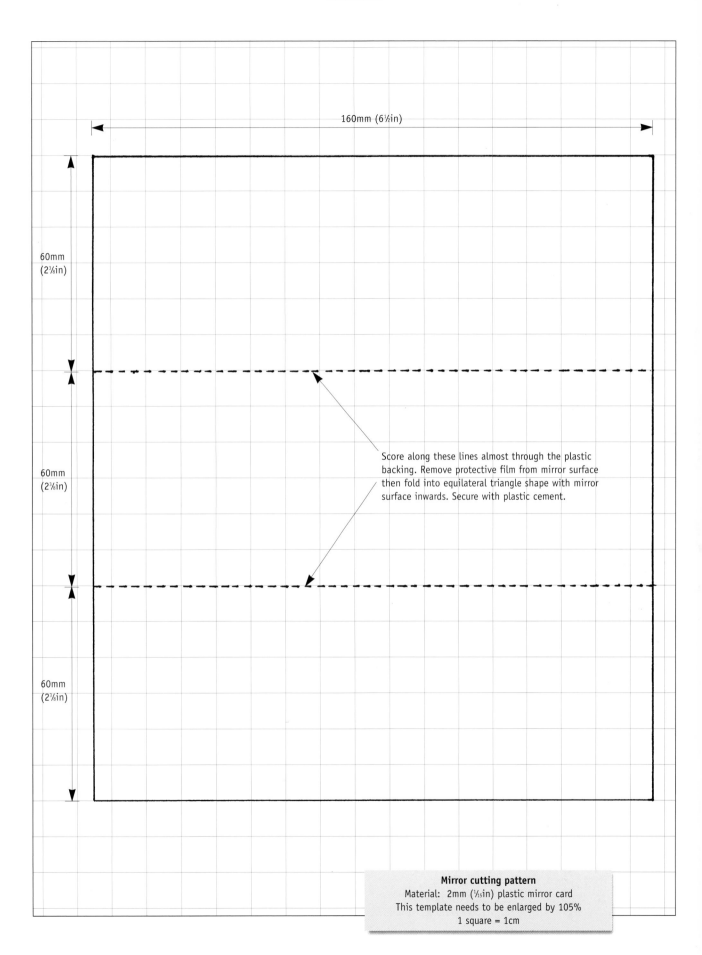

160mm (6½in)

60mm (2⅜in)

60mm (2⅜in)

60mm (2⅜in)

Score along these lines almost through the plastic backing. Remove protective film from mirror surface then fold into equilateral triangle shape with mirror surface inwards. Secure with plastic cement.

Mirror cutting pattern
Material: 2mm (⅛in) plastic mirror card
This template needs to be enlarged by 105%
1 square = 1cm

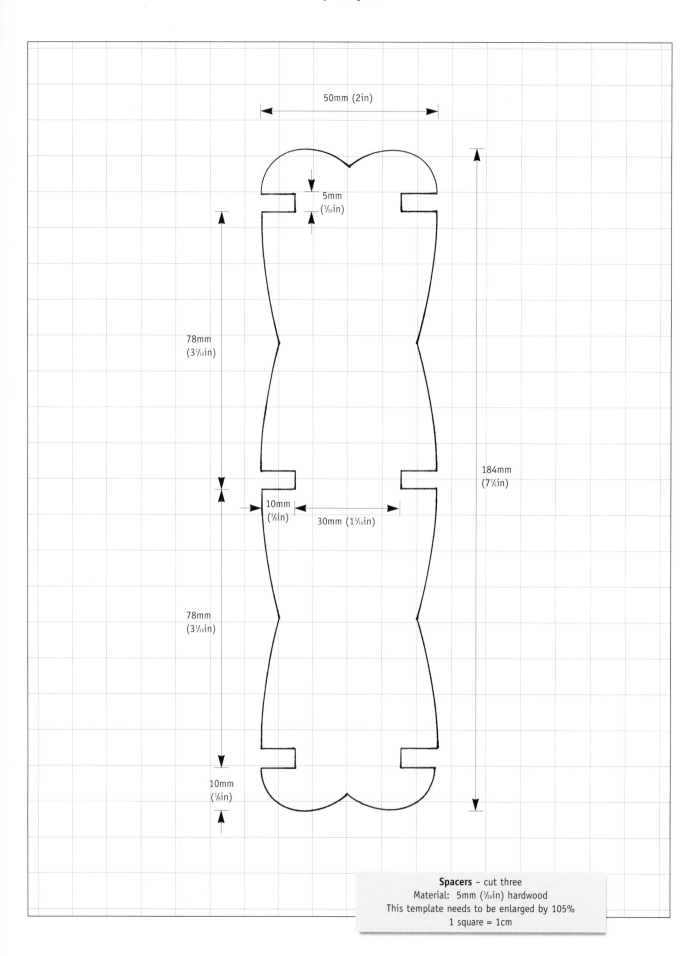

50mm (2in)

5mm
(³⁄₁₆in)

78mm
(3¹⁄₁₆in)

184mm
(7¼in)

10mm
(³⁄₈in)

30mm (1³⁄₁₆in)

78mm
(3¹⁄₁₆in)

10mm
(³⁄₈in)

Spacers – cut three
Material: 5mm (³⁄₁₆in) hardwood
This template needs to be enlarged by 105%
1 square = 1cm

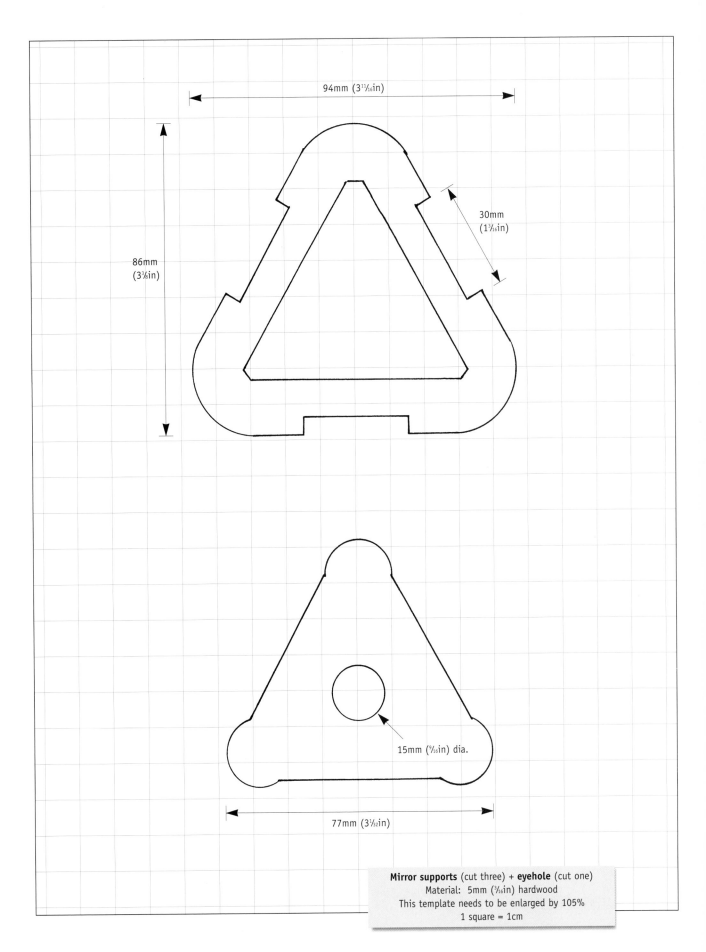

94mm (3¹¹⁄₁₆in)

86mm
(3⅜in)

30mm
(1³⁄₁₆in)

15mm (⁹⁄₁₆in) dia.

77mm (3¹⁄₃₂in)

Mirror supports (cut three) + **eyehole** (cut one)
Material: 5mm (³⁄₁₆in) hardwood
This template needs to be enlarged by 105%
1 square = 1cm

Finger plates for a door

These finger plates add a decorative touch to a plain door but they are functional, too, as they help protect the door from sticky fingers.

To ensure the finished set does not protrude too much from the door, use a fairly thin hardwood such as the 4mm (³⁄₁₆in) iroko, which was used here. Other materials could of course be used, and then decorated to suit personal preferences.

The completed finger plates installed on a door

Setting up the cutting pattern on the material to be used to make the finger plates

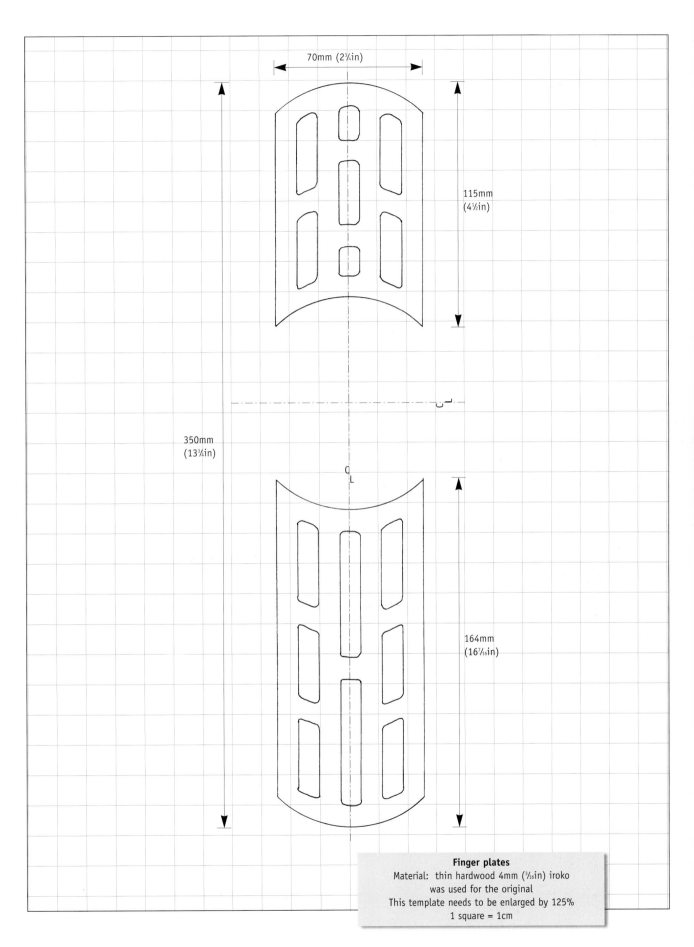

70mm (2¾in)

115mm
(4½in)

C
L

C
L

350mm
(13¾in)

164mm
(16⁷⁄₁₆in)

Finger plates
Material: thin hardwood 4mm (³⁄₁₆in) iroko
was used for the original
This template needs to be enlarged by 125%
1 square = 1cm

Decorative border for frame

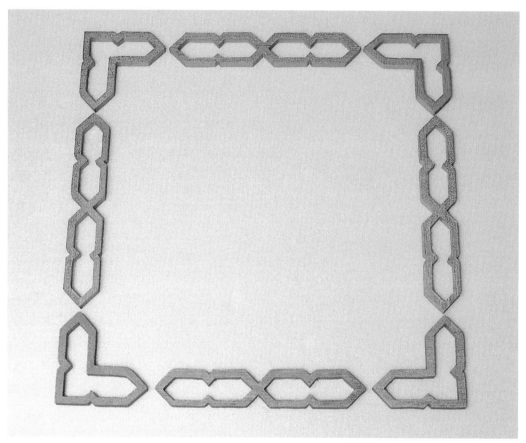

The set of items cut out and finished in bronze

This pattern provides both straight section patterns and a matching corner design for decorating a plain picture frame.

Corners are usually needed in sets of four but you could consider a part design using just two straight patterns and one corner, or any other combination that takes your fancy.

The patterns can be adapted to suit your needs, so just measure up to decide how many straight pieces you will need before cutting out.

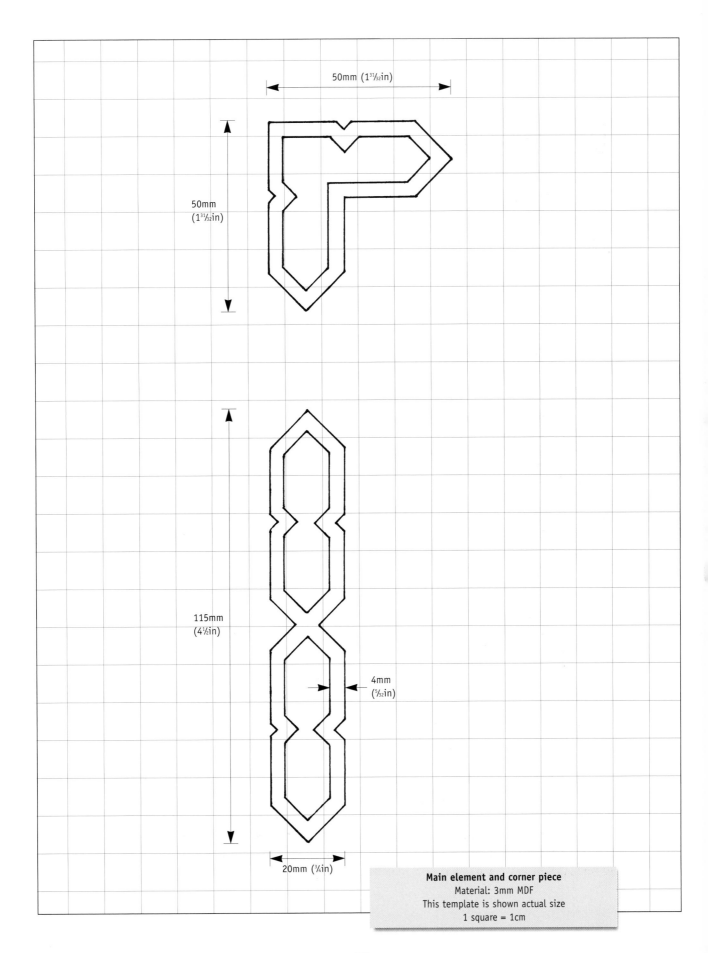

50mm (1³¹⁄₃₂in)

50mm
(1³¹⁄₃₂in)

115mm
(4½in)

4mm
(⁵⁄₃₂in)

20mm (¾in)

Main element and corner piece
Material: 3mm MDF
This template is shown actual size
1 square = 1cm

Decorative bows

The completed bows – a corner type is used here to decorate a standard ring binder

This gingerbread item can add a decorative touch to almost anything, from book covers to furniture – just scale it up or down to suit a particular application. The parts are cut out individually from thin sheet material, rounded off, and then simply glued in place wherever they are required.

It is helpful to photocopy an extra cutting pattern, so that the spare can be used to identify the positioning of the different bow parts as you work.

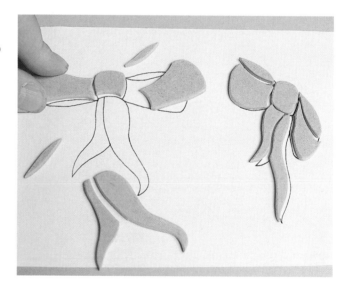

Two patterns have been used here, one for the corner and the other for positioning the design

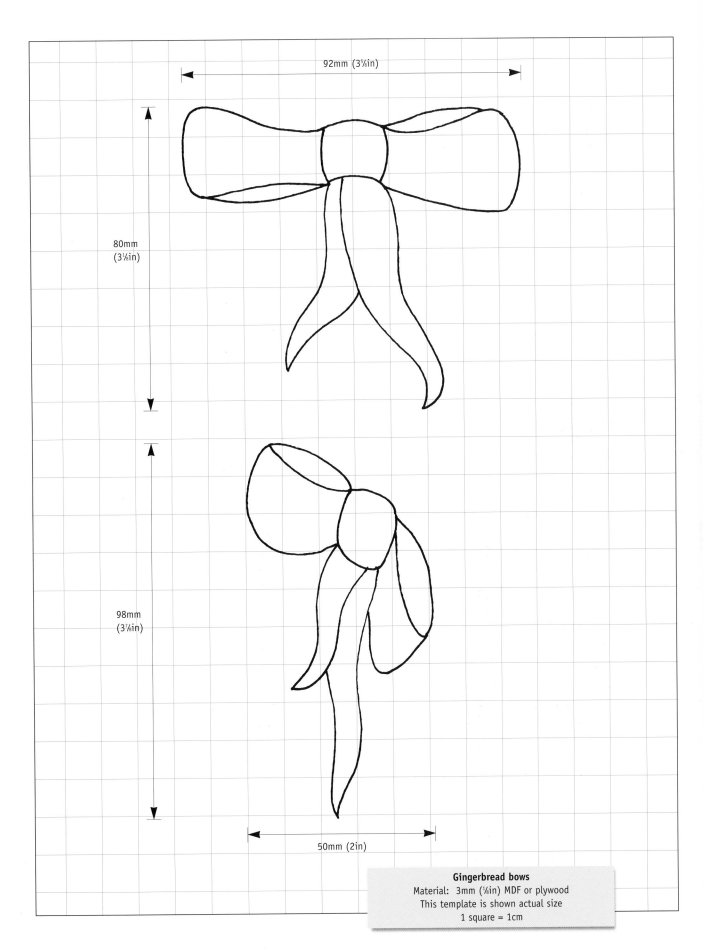

92mm (3⅝in)

80mm
(3⅛in)

98mm
(3⅞in)

50mm (2in)

Gingerbread bows
Material: 3mm (⅛in) MDF or plywood
This template is shown actual size
1 square = 1cm

Metric conversion table

inches to millimetres

inches	mm	inches	mm	inches	mm
⅛	3	9	229	30	762
¼	6	10	254	31	787
⅜	10	11	279	32	813
½	13	12	305	33	838
⅝	16	13	330	34	864
¾	19	14	356	35	889
⅞	22	15	381	36	914
1	25	16	406	37	940
1¼	32	17	432	38	965
1½	38	18	457	39	991
1¾	44	19	483	40	1016
2	51	20	508	41	1041
2½	64	21	533	42	1067
3	76	22	559	43	1092
3½	89	23	584	44	1118
4	102	24	610	45	1143
4½	114	25	635	46	1168
5	127	26	660	47	1194
6	152	27	686	48	1219
7	178	28	711	49	1245
8	203	29	737	50	1270

About the author

John Everett is a technical artist and photographer with a long-standing interest in woodwork and other crafts. He lives and works in Wales, where he produces craft kits and projects for a range of individuals and organizations, including schools and colleges.

He is a regular contributor to craft magazines, and author of three other books published by GMC Publications, *The Scrollsaw: Twenty Projects*; *Minidrill: Fifteen Projects*; and *Glass Engraving Pattern Book*.

GMC Publications
BOOKS

WOODCARVING

The Art of the Woodcarver	GMC Publications
Carving Architectural Detail in Wood:	
The Classical Tradition	Frederick Wilbur
Carving Birds & Beasts	GMC Publications
Carving Nature: Wildlife Studies in Wood	Frank Fox-Wilson
Carving on Turning	Chris Pye
Carving Realistic Birds	David Tippey
Decorative Woodcarving	Jeremy Williams
Elements of Woodcarving	Chris Pye
Essential Tips for Woodcarvers	GMC Publications
Essential Woodcarving Techniques	Dick Onians
Further Useful Tips for Woodcarvers	GMC Publications
Lettercarving in Wood: A Practical Course	Chris Pye
Making & Using Working Drawings for Realistic Model Animals	
	Basil Fordham
Power Tools for Woodcarving	David Tippey
Practical Tips for Turners & Carvers	GMC Publications
Relief Carving in Wood: A Practical Introduction	Chris Pye
Understanding Woodcarving	GMC Publications
Understanding Woodcarving in the Round	GMC Publications
Useful Techniques for Woodcarvers	GMC Publications
Wildfowl Carving – Volume 1	Jim Pearce
Wildfowl Carving – Volume 2	Jim Pearce
The Woodcarvers	GMC Publications
Woodcarving: A Complete Course	Ron Butterfield
Woodcarving: A Foundation Course	Zoë Gertner
Woodcarving for Beginners	GMC Publications
Woodcarving Tools & Equipment Test Reports	GMC Publications
Woodcarving Tools, Materials & Equipment	Chris Pye

WOODTURNING

Adventures in Woodturning	David Springett
Bert Marsh: Woodturner	Bert Marsh
Bill Jones' Notes from the Turning Shop	Bill Jones
Bill Jones' Further Notes from the Turning Shop	Bill Jones
Bowl Turning Techniques Masterclass	Tony Boase
Colouring Techniques for Woodturners	Jan Sanders
The Craftsman Woodturner	Peter Child
Decorative Techniques for Woodturners	Hilary Bowen
Faceplate Turning	GMC Publications
Fun at the Lathe	R.C. Bell
Further Useful Tips for Woodturners	GMC Publications
Illustrated Woodturning Techniques	John Hunnex
Intermediate Woodturning Projects	GMC Publications
Keith Rowley's Woodturning Projects	Keith Rowley
Multi-Centre Woodturning	Ray Hopper
Practical Tips for Turners & Carvers	GMC Publications

Spindle Turning	GMC Publications
Turning Green Wood	Michael O'Donnell
Turning Miniatures in Wood	John Sainsbury
Turning Pens and Pencils	Kip Christensen & Rex Burningham
Turning Wooden Toys	Terry Lawrence
Understanding Woodturning	Ann & Bob Phillips
Useful Techniques for Woodturners	GMC Publications
Useful Woodturning Projects	GMC Publications
Woodturning: Bowls, Platters, Hollow Forms, Vases, Vessels, Bottles, Flasks, Tankards, Plates	GMC Publications
Woodturning: A Foundation Course (New Edition)	Keith Rowley
Woodturning: A Fresh Approach	Robert Chapman
Woodturning: An Individual Approach	Dave Regester
Woodturning: A Source Book of Shapes	John Hunnex
Woodturning Jewellery	Hilary Bowen
Woodturning Masterclass	Tony Boase
Woodturning Techniques	GMC Publications
Woodturning Tools & Equipment Test Reports	GMC Publications
Woodturning Wizardry	David Springett

WOODWORKING

Bird Boxes and Feeders for the Garden	Dave Mackenzie
Complete Woodfinishing	Ian Hosker
David Charlesworth's Furniture-Making Techniques	David Charlesworth
Furniture & Cabinetmaking Projects	GMC Publications
Furniture-Making Projects for the Wood Craftsman	GMC Publications
Furniture-Making Techniques for the Wood Craftsman	GMC Publications
Furniture Projects	Rod Wales
Furniture Restoration (Practical Crafts)	Kevin Jan Bonner
Furniture Restoration and Repair for Beginners	Kevin Jan Bonner
Furniture Restoration Workshop	Kevin Jan Bonner
Green Woodwork	Mike Abbott
Making & Modifying Woodworking Tools	Jim Kingshott
Making Chairs and Tables	GMC Publications
Making Classic English Furniture	Paul Richardson
Making Fine Furniture	Tom Darby
Making Little Boxes from Wood	John Bennett
Making Shaker Furniture	Barry Jackson
Making Woodwork Aids and Devices	Robert Wearing
Minidrill: Fifteen Projects	John Everett
Pine Furniture Projects for the Home	Dave Mackenzie
Router Magic: Jigs, Fixtures and Tricks to Unleash your Router's Full Potential	Bill Hylton
Routing for Beginners	Anthony Bailey
Scrollsaw Pattern Book	John Everett
The Scrollsaw: Twenty Projects	John Everett
Sharpening: The Complete Guide	Jim Kingshott
Sharpening Pocket Reference Book	Jim Kingshott
Space-Saving Furniture Projects	Dave Mackenzie

Stickmaking: A Complete Course   *Andrew Jones & Clive George*
Stickmaking Handbook   *Andrew Jones & Clive George*
Test Reports: *The Router* and *Furniture & Cabinetmaking*   *GMC Publications*
Veneering: A Complete Course   *Ian Hosker*
Woodfinishing Handbook (Practical Crafts) *Ian Hosker*
Woodworking with the Router: Professional
  Router Techniques any Woodworker can Use   *Bill Hylton & Fred Matlack*
The Workshop   *Jim Kingshott*

UPHOLSTERY

Seat Weaving (Practical Crafts)   *Ricky Holdstock*
The Upholsterer's Pocket Reference Book   *David James*
Upholstery: A Complete Course (Revised Edition)   *David James*
Upholstery Restoration   *David James*
Upholstery Techniques & Projects   *David James*
Upholstery Tips and Hints   *David James*

TOYMAKING

Designing & Making Wooden Toys   *Terry Kelly*
Fun to Make Wooden Toys & Games   *Jeff & Jennie Loader*
Making Wooden Toys & Games   *Jeff & Jennie Loader*
Restoring Rocking Horses   *Clive Green & Anthony Dew*
Scrollsaw Toy Projects   *Ivor Carlyle*
Scrollsaw Toys for All Ages   *Ivor Carlyle*
Wooden Toy Projects   *GMC Publications*

DOLLS' HOUSES AND MINIATURES

Architecture for Dolls' Houses   *Joyce Percival*
A Beginners' Guide to the Dolls' House Hobby   *Jean Nisbett*
The Complete Dolls' House Book   *Jean Nisbett*
The Dolls' House 1/24 Scale: A Complete Introduction   *Jean Nisbett*
Dolls' House Accessories, Fixtures and Fittings   *Andrea Barham*
Dolls' House Bathrooms: Lots of Little Loos   *Patricia King*
Dolls' House Fireplaces and Stoves   *Patricia King*
Easy to Make Dolls' House Accessories   *Andrea Barham*
Heraldic Miniature Knights   *Peter Greenhill*
Make Your Own Dolls' House Furniture   *Maurice Harper*
Making Dolls' House Furniture   *Patricia King*
Making Georgian Dolls' Houses   *Derek Rowbottom*
Making Miniature Gardens   *Freida Gray*
Making Miniature Oriental Rugs & Carpets *Meik & Ian McNaughton*
Making Period Dolls' House Accessories   *Andrea Barham*
Making 1/12 Scale Character Figures   *James Carrington*
Making Tudor Dolls' Houses   *Derek Rowbottom*
Making Victorian Dolls' House Furniture   *Patricia King*
Miniature Bobbin Lace   *Roz Snowden*
Miniature Embroidery for the Georgian Dolls' House   *Pamela Warner*
Miniature Embroidery for the Victorian Dolls' House *Pamela Warner*
Miniature Needlepoint Carpets   *Janet Granger*
More Miniature Oriental Rugs & Carpets   *Meik & Ian McNaughton*
The Secrets of the Dolls' House Makers   *Jean Nisbett*

CRAFTS

American Patchwork Designs in Needlepoint *Melanie Tacon*
A Beginners' Guide to Rubber Stamping   *Brenda Hunt*
Blackwork: A New Approach   *Brenda Day*
Celtic Cross Stitch Designs   *Carol Phillipson*
Celtic Knotwork Designs   *Sheila Sturrock*
Celtic Knotwork Handbook   *Sheila Sturrock*
Celtic Spirals and Other Designs   *Sheila Sturrock*
Collage from Seeds, Leaves and Flowers   *Joan Carver*
Complete Pyrography   *Stephen Poole*
Contemporary Smocking   *Dorothea Hall*
Creating Colour with Dylon   *Dylon International*
Creating Knitwear Designs   *Pat Ashforth & Steve Plummer*
Creative Doughcraft   *Patricia Hughes*
Creative Embroidery Techniques Using Colour
  Through Gold   *Daphne J. Ashby & Jackie Woolsey*
The Creative Quilter: Techniques and Projects   *Pauline Brown*
Cross Stitch Kitchen Projects   *Janet Granger*
Cross Stitch on Colour   *Sheena Rogers*
Decorative Beaded Purses   *Enid Taylor*
Designing and Making Cards   *Glennis Gilruth*
Embroidery Tips & Hints   *Harold Hayes*
Glass Painting   *Emma Sedman*
How to Arrange Flowers: A Japanese Approach
  to English Design   *Taeko Marvelly*
An Introduction to Crewel Embroidery   *Mave Glenny*
Making and Using Working Drawings for Realistic
  Model Animals   *Basil F. Fordham*
Making Character Bears   *Valerie Tyler*
Making Decorative Screens   *Amanda Howes*
Making Greetings Cards for Beginners   *Pat Sutherland*
Making Hand-Sewn Boxes: Techniques and Projects   *Jackie Woolsey*
Making Knitwear Fit   *Pat Ashforth & Steve Plummer*
Natural Ideas for Christmas: Fantastic
  Decorations to Make   *Josie Cameron-Ashcroft & Carol Cox*
Needlepoint: A Foundation Course   *Sandra Hardy*
Needlepoint 1/12 Scale: Design Collections for the Dolls' House   *Felicity Price*
Pyrography Designs   *Norma Gregory*
Pyrography Handbook (Practical Crafts)   *Stephen Poole*
Ribbons and Roses   *Lee Lockheed*
Rosewindows for Quilters   *Angela Besley*
Rubber Stamping with Other Crafts   *Lynne Garner*
Sponge Painting   *Ann Rooney*
Tassel Making for Beginners   *Enid Taylor*
Tatting Collage   *Lindsay Rogers*
Temari: A Traditional Japanese Embroidery Technique   *Margaret Ludlow*
Theatre Models in Paper and Card   *Robert Burgess*
Wool Embroidery and Design   *Lee Lockheed*

GARDENING

Auriculas for Everyone: How to Grow and Show
  Perfect Plants   *Mary Robinson*
Bird Boxes and Feeders for the Garden   *Dave Mackenzie*
The Birdwatcher's Garden   *Hazel & Pamela Johnson*

VIDEOS

MAGAZINES

WOODTURNING ◆ WOODCARVING ◆ FURNITURE & CABINETMAKING
THE DOLLS' HOUSE MAGAZINE
THE ROUTER ◆ BUSINESSMATTERS
WATER GARDENING ◆ EXOTIC GARDENING
GARDEN CALENDAR
OUTDOOR PHOTOGRAPHY ◆ WOODWORKING

The above represents a full list of all titles currently published or scheduled to be published.
All are available direct from the Publishers or through bookshops, newsagents and specialist retailers.
To place an order, or to obtain a complete catalogue, contact:

**GMC Publications,
Castle Place, 166 High Street, Lewes,
East Sussex BN7 1XU, United Kingdom
Tel: 01273 488005 Fax: 01273 478606
e-mail: pubs@thegmcgroup.com**

Orders by credit card are accepted